OFFICIAL APPOINTMENT.

HEADQUARTERS OF THE NATIONAL COMMITTEE,
CHICAGO, May 19, 1868.

At a session of the National Executive Committee, this day held, it was

"*Resolved*, That Messrs. Ely, Burnham and Bartlett, Official Reporters of the "Courts of Chicago, be hereby appointed the Official Reporters of the proceedings "of the National Union Republican Convention, to be held at the City of Chicago "on Wednesday, the 20th day of May, at 12 M., for the purpose of nominating "candidates for the offices of President and Vice President of the United States."

MARCUS L. WARD, OF NEW JERSEY,
Chairman.

JNO. D. DEFREES, OF INDIANA,
Secretary.

PRESIDENTIAL ELECTION, 1868.

PROCEEDINGS

OF THE

NATIONAL UNION

REPUBLICAN CONVENTION,

HELD AT

CHICAGO, MAY 20 AND 21, 1868.

REPORTED BY ELY, BURNHAM & BARTLETT, CHICAGO,
OFFICIAL REPORTERS OF THE CONVENTION.

CHICAGO:
EVENING JOURNAL PRINT, No. 46 DEARBORN STREET.

NATIONAL UNION REPUBLICAN CONVENTION.

WEDNESDAY, May 20, 1868.

The National Union Republican Convention, to nominate candidates for the offices of President and Vice President of the United States, assembled in Crosby's Opera House, Chicago, Illinois, at 12 M., in response to the following call:

NATIONAL UNION REPUBLICAN CONVENTION.

The undersigned, constituting the National Committee designated by the Convention held at Baltimore on the 7th of June, 1864, do appoint that a Convention of the Union Republican party be held at the City of Chicago, on Wednesday, the 20th day of May next, at 12 o'clock M., for the purpose of nominating candidates for the offices of President and Vice President of the United States.

Each State in the United States is authorized to be represented in said Convention by a number of delegates equal to twice the number of Senators and Representatives to which each State is entitled in the National Congress.

We invite the co-operation of all citizens who rejoice that our great civil war has happily terminated in the discomfiture of rebellion; who would hold fast the unity and integrity of the Republic, and maintain its paramount right to defend to the utmost its existence, whether imperiled by a secret conspiracy or armed force; of an economical administration of the public expenditures; of the complete extirpation of the principles and policy of slavery, and of the speedy re-organization of those States whose governments were destroyed by the rebellion, and the permanent restoration to their proper practical relations with the United States, in accordance with the true principles of a republican government.

MARCUS L. WARD, of New Jersey, Chairman.

JNO. D. DEFREES, of Indiana, Secretary.

J. B. CLARK, New Hampshire,
A. B. GARDNER, Vermont.
S. A. PURVIANCE, Pennsylvania.
B. C. COOK, Illinois.
D. B. STUBBS, Iowa.
H. C. HOFFMAN, Maryland.
W. J. COWING, Virginia.
C. L. ROBINSON, Florida.
HORACE GREELEY, New York,
B. R. COWEN, Ohio.
N. EDMUNDS, Dakota,
THOS. G. TURNER, Rhode Island.
S. J. BOWEN, District of Columbia.
S. F. HERSEY, Maine.
WM. CLAFLIN, Massachusetts.
J. S. FOWLER, Tennessee.
MARSH GIDDINGS, Michigan.
A. W. CAMPBELL, West Virginia.
N. B. SMITHERS, Delaware.
W. A. PILE, Missouri.
S. JUDD, Wisconsin.
H. H. STARKWEATHER, Connecticut.
WM. WINDOM, Minnesota.
D. R. GOODLOE, North Carolina.
SAMUEL CRAWFORD, Kansas.
J. P. CHAFFEE, Colorado.

CONVENTION CALLED TO ORDER.

Gov. Marcus L. Ward, of New Jersey, Chairman of the National Executive Committee, called the Convention to order at the prescribed hour, and spoke as follows:

Delegates to the National Convention of the Union Republican Party—You have assembled at the call of the National Convention to nominate its standard-bearers for the ensuing campaign; to declare your unswerving attachment to union and liberty; and to pledge that you will take no step backward in the work of reconstructing the rebel States and re-establishing the Union. [Applause.]

You are here to bear witness that the war, so gallantly and so gloriously waged for the life of the nation, was not a failure. You are here to point to a Republic boundless in extent and resources, guarded and protected by one common flag, and upheld by a patriotic and loyal people. [Applause.]

An emancipated race has been lifted from the debasement of slavery, and, to-day, with the Union men of the South, re-organizes, in the name of liberty, the Governments and institutions of the rebellious States. The history of the Republican party is a record of the true progress of the nation. It has successively met and conquered all those hostile parties represented by the effete ideas and perishing institutions of the past, and it must now determine to vindicate anew its measures and its policy, by the wisdom and courage which plan, and the determination and labor which organize, victory. In this spirit you are here assembled to perform the responsible duties assigned you, and I doubt not your action will meet the approval of the vast constituency you represent. The nation understands that neither armed treason nor political treachery can arrest the triumph of our cause and the success of our candidates. [Great applause, and display of national flags.]

If, as indicated by the unanimity of feeling which prevails, you shall designate as our leader the great captain of the age, [great applause,] whose brilliant achievements in the field have been equaled by his wisdom in the Cabinet, [applause,] the nation will greet it as the precursor of victory to our cause and of peace to the Republic. [Loud applause.]

Bishop Simpson will offer prayer.

PRAYER.

Matthew Simpson, D. D., then offered the following prayer:

Oh, Lord, our Lord, how excellent is Thy name in all the earth! Thou art the King of Kings and Lord of Lords. Thou hast laid the foundation of the earth, and Thy hands have formed the heavens. We praise Thee for all Thy mercies Thou hast conferred upon us as individuals, as communities, and as a nation. While we deplore our manifold sins, we bless Thee for life and for reason, for a glorious revelation, the gift of Thy Son, our Saviour, and for the hope of a blissful immortality. As a nation, we praise Thee for the goodly heritage which Thou hast given us—so vast in extent, so immense in its resources. We praise Thee for the deeds to which Thou didst inspire our fathers, and the precious memories which they have left to us. We thank Thee for the institutions with which our land has been blessed—for our civil and religious liberties. We thank Thee for the right to meet and deliberate; we bless Thee for the freedom which breathes through all classes of society, and especially we praise Thee, Oh, our Father and our God, that in the midst of all our trials Thou hast ever been with our nation. Though we have been chastised because of our sins, and we would humble us in Thy presence because of our sins, yet we bless Thee that, whilst Thou hast chastised, Thou hast also poured blessings upon us.

While we remember that multiplied thousands have recently fallen in the fierce struggles which have been in our land, we bless Thee that the storm-cloud has passed away; that the voice of battle has been hushed; that peace has been restored to our borders again; and, notwithstanding all our trials, we bless Thy holy name, that Thou hast made us, as we believe, stronger and firmer than ever before. As the tree is strengthened by the storms of winter, and prepared for the verdure of coming spring and summer, so we trust Thou hast prepared our nation, by the trials through which we have passed, for the glorious future into which we are about to enter.

We ask Thee that Thy blessing still be with us, as a nation. Bless, we pray Thee, all our rulers. May Thy benediction rest upon the President of the United States, and upon all associated with him in authority, upon the Senate and House of Representatives, upon the officers of our army and navy, and upon the Governors and Legislators of our various Commonwealths, and upon all those who are in authority in all the departments of our Government.

Be in them a spirit of wisdom. Be in them a spirit of grace. May they rule with a view to the prosperity of the nation and an eye to Thy glory. And as it is in Thy hand alone to raise up and to perpetuate kingdoms, we pray that this, our nation, may be ever precious in Thy sight.

Our Father and our God, we acknowledge that we are ever in Thy hand; that all plans without Thee are futile, and all arrangements without Thee are vain. And now, upon this Assembly, convened from all parts of the Union, may Thy special blessing rest. Have them in Thy holy keeping. May the spirit of harmony and wisdom prevail in their councils, and may such results be reached as Thou shalt approve, and as shall lead to the prosperity and the perpetuity and the glory of our beloved land. Almighty God, we beseech Thee so to direct in all events that may happen, that the greatest possible good may be worked out. We do thank Thee that Thou rulest in all nations and in all agencies, and in all perils, and though there may be night for a season the light cometh in the morning; though there may be the storms of winter, there shall succeed the sweetness of the breath of spring; though there may sometimes be clouds which in our view seem dark, and lowering, and gloomy, it is in Thy hand to cause all to pass away as the mists of the morning and the clear light again to shine.

God of our fathers, be with us, their sons, as Thou wast with them. May Thy benediction be upon all parts of the country here represented; and when these citizens shall return to their homes, may they find every interest in peace and in prosperity. We thank Thee that here all parts of our nation are represented. We thank Thee that the North meets with the South, and the East meets with the West. We thank Thee that citizens of all classes and pursuits are here convened. We bless Thee that freedom has diffused its healthful influences over the land, and that the

States so lately in rebellion are being successfully reconstructed in peace and prosperity. Hasten the work so gloriously commenced; may there be nothing that shall mar its progress. And, Oh, hasten the moment when all parts of our land shall be firmly and intimately, and fraternally, and perpetually bound together in one common bond of union, and this dear land of ours shall be, as we believe Thou hast designed it to be, a light to all the nations of the earth that shall throw its rays across the Atlantic to Europe, and across the Pacific to Asia, until the dark places of Africa shall have been made glad and the islands of the sea take up the song of praise, and a human brotherhood shall be formed vast as the globe on which we dwell, and sentiments of love, and duty, and adoration shall inspire our common humanity, and prepare it for that glorious assemblage that shall one day convene before the throne of God.

Hear us while we would unite in praying, as Thou hast taught us, saying:

Our Father which art in Heaven, hallowed be Thy name. Thy kingdom come. Thy will be done in earth, as it is in Heaven. Give us this day our daily bread, and forgive us our trespasses as we forgive those who trespass against us. Lead us not into temptation, but deliver us from evil: for Thine is the kingdom, and the power, and the glory forever and ever. Amen.

ELECTION OF TEMPORARY CHAIRMAN.

CHAIRMAN OF THE NATIONAL COMMITTEE [MR. WARD, of New Jersey,]—By direction of the National Committee, I nominate Carl Schurz, of Missouri, as temporary chairman of this Convention. [Repeated cheers.] As many of you as favor the adoption of this nomination will say "aye."

The nomination unanimously prevailed.

CHAIRMAN OF THE NATIONAL COMMITTEE—I will designate Mr. Tremain, of New York, and Mr. Thompson, of Indiana, to wait upon General Schurz and conduct that gentleman to the chair.

On being conducted to the chair, Mr. Schurz was received with great enthusiasm, and was presented to the Convention by the Chairman of the National Committee.

ADDRESS BY GEN. SCHURZ.

MR. SCHURZ, of Missouri—Gentlemen of the Convention—It is difficult for me to express how highly I appreciate the honor you have conferred upon me by this nomination. You will permit me to offer you my sincerest thanks.

This is the fourth National Convention of the Republican party. The short career of this party has been marked by events to which coming generations will point with pride, admiration and gratitude. The Republican party was born a giant. [Applause.] In its very infancy it grappled with the prejudice of race, which, until then, seemed to be omnipotent with the masses of the American people.

Our second onset broke through it, and carried the immortal Abraham Lincoln into the Executive Chair of the Republic—[great applause]—as the great champion of the anti-slavery cause. [Prolonged applause.]

Then came the slaveholders' rebellion, and, under Republican leadership, the loyal people of this country displayed a noble heroism and self-sacrificing devotion and perseverance, under obstacles and defeat, which may well serve as a glorious example to all nations of the earth. [Applause.]

The result of the struggle corresponds with the great effort. The life of the nation has been saved; the dark blot of slavery has been wiped from our national escutcheon [applause]; four millions of bondsmen have been raised from the dust and from their ancient degradation; the outraged dignity of human nature has been gloriously vindicated; and this day, those States, the peculiar condition of which was but recently a disgrace to the American name, return to us under the national banner, which, now, at last, is to them what it ought ever to have been—the great emblem of impartial justice, of universal liberty, and of equal rights.

All these things have been accomplished under Republican auspices, and without indulging in vain self-glorification, it may be truly said that the history of the Republican party is closely identified with the noblest achievements of this century. [Applause.]

But there are new problems equally great before us; we have to secure the results of the great struggle against the dangers of reaction; we have to adapt the laws and institutions of this country to the new order of things.

The solution of that problem will require no less enthusiasm, no less devotion, no less perseverance, than the struggles which lie behind us.

It will require more. It will require that calm statesmanship which consists in a clear appreciation of the objects to be attained, and a thorough knowledge of the means by which they can be accomplished.

When the Republican party was about to enter upon the creative part of its mission, it was, by one of the most atrocious crimes ever recorded in history, deprived of the man whose highest virtue as a ruler consisted in his always acting upon the noblest impulses of the popular heart. Abraham Lincoln was struck down in the fulness of his glory, and we are left now to measure the greatness of our loss by what he left behind him in his place. [Laughter.]

Then began, for us, the time of disappointments and of unexpected trials. Our policy was thwarted by the very man, who, in an unfortunate hour, we had put upon the road to power. The legislative and executive departments of the Government were pitted against one another in a fierce struggle. New dangers were looming up where there ought to have been a quiet and peaceable development.

We have had our hours of painful experience, but what of that? Are we the men to be disturbed by the mere appearance of danger? Are not the principles which we advocate just as great as they ever were? Is not the necessity of their realization just as apparent as ever? Is not justice still justice, right still right, and truth still truth? Are we not defenders of justice, right and truth, to-day, as we were yesterday? What, then, is there to frighten the most pusillanimous?

Victory will be true to the Republican party as long as the Republican party is true to itself. [Cheers.]

What we have to do is clear. Let us fix our eyes firmly upon the noble ends to be attained, and not permit our equanimity to be disturbed by an untoward accident. [Applause.] Let not the passions inflamed by the stinging disappointment of this hour, however keen our sense of wrong may be, carry us beyond the bounds of wisdom and of self-respect. [Applause.] The things we have to accomplish are so great that, whatever the provocation may be, we can certainly not afford to let personal resentments seduce us into compromising the high dignity of our cause. [Cheers.]

Whoever may be our friends, whoever may become our enemies, let us march on with the unflinching determination to perform all the duties incumbent upon us, to secure justice to the soldiers who fought our battles [applause]; justice to the Southern Union man, who, for the national cause, imperiled his life and fortune [cheers]; justice to the colored race, to whom we have promised true liberty forever [great applause]; justice to then ational creditor, who staked his credit upon the good faith of the American people. [Applause.]

Let us faithfully strive to restore the honor of the Government, to crush corruption wherever we find it, inside of the party, just as well as outside of it [loud applause], and to place the public service of the country in the hands of honest, true and capable men. [Cheers.] Let us, with unshaken purpose, work out the manifest logic of the results already gained for liberty and equal rights; let us fearlessly acknowledge that the career of the Republican party will not be ended till the great trusts proclaimed in the Declaration of Independence, in the fullest meaning of the term, have become a living reality on every inch of American soil. [Loud applause.]

Yes, let us be true to our history, true to ourselves, and fear nothing. No step backward. Onward is the charm-word of victory. [Cheers.] Let us see again the banner of progress, of liberty, of equal rights, of national faith, nailed to the very top of the mast. [Cheers.] And I spurn the idea that the American people could ever so far forget themselves as to throw their destiny into the hands of men who, but yesterday, strove to destroy the Republic, and who, to-day, stand ready to dishonor it. [Cheers.]

TEMPORARY SECRETARIES.

MR. SMITHERS, of Delaware—Mr. Chairman, to effect the preliminary organization, I move that the following gentlemen be appointed temporary Secretaries: B. R. Cowen, of Ohio; Luther Caldwell, of New York, and F. S. Richards, of Tennessee.

The motion prevailed.

THE CHAIRMAN—What is the further pleasure of the Convention? I think it has been customary that each delegation should present one of their number as a member of a Committee on Credentials.

COMMITTEE ON CREDENTIALS.

MR. SMITHERS, of Delaware—Mr. Chairman, I move you, sir, that a Committee on Credentials be appointed, consisting of one from each delegation in the Convention.

THE CHAIRMAN—Gentlemen, you have heard the motion.

MR. ———, of ———.—I suggest, Mr. Chairman, that the Secretary call the list of States, and that each respective delegation shall name a gentleman who will constitute a committee on their part.

MR. SMITHERS, of Delaware—I made that motion as suggested by gentlemen around me, and which I thought to be proper. I will modify the motion in accordance with the rule which has been heretofore adopted. As I understand, there are two States—Maryland and California—in which the delegations are contested. I therefore modify my motion so that these States be omitted, and that their claims be decided by the Committee on Credentials.

The Secretary called the State of California, and the delegation named Mr. P. E. Conner.

The Secretary called the State of Connecticut, and the delegation named Mr. Wm. G. Coe.

MR. SMITHERS, of Delaware—Mr. Chairman, there seems to be some misunderstanding. I understood that the States in which the delegates were contested were to be omitted. Is it so?

THE CHAIRMAN—I will state to the Convention that, as the name of each State is called, one member of the delegation from that State will rise and indicate the choice of the delegation from that State as a member of the Committee on Credentials.

MR. SMITHERS, of Delaware—Then I was right at first, Mr. Chairman, and my suggestion comes in properly, that California and Maryland shall be omitted from that committee.

MR. SEARS, of California—Mr. Chairman, as the gentleman has mentioned the State which I in part represent, I wish to deny that there is any contest whatever in regard to the State of California. It is true, sir, that there is a man here who has been before the Executive Committee claiming to contest our seats; but, sir, there is one man only—

MR. VAN ZANDT, of Rhode Island—Mr. Chairman, I rise to a point of order. The matter should be referred to the Committee on Credentials.

MR. SEARS, of California—Mr. Chairman, I ask but two minutes to make an explanation. [Cries—"Go on," "go on," "hear him!"] We do not desire to bring this contest up here, but the gentleman has forced it upon us.

Now, sir, the man who here contests our seats, or tries to contest our seats, voted the Copperhead ticket at the last election in California. ["Hear, hear." "Put him out!" "Out with him!"] He and one or two others met in a back room and selected delegates to attend this Convention. They have no party; they have had no primary election; they had no Convention; they had nothing, sir; and I believe, in my humble judgment, that he comes here, and that his passage is paid by Democratic money, to keep up this division in our State. ["That's so." Hisses and applause.]

Now, sir, we are here representing the Union Republican party of California.

We polled forty thousand loyal votes in that State at the last election, [applause], and the sneaking, crawling squad, which this man represents, only polled two thousand, and out of that two thousand, in our last Convention, they could not find in all the State of California ten men who would accept of this position which he occupies. [Laughter.] They selected men who had formerly lived in California. Two of them are in your city, and came into our rooms last night and repudiated the entire proceeding, and said they were for us. Therefore, sir, this man stands alone in attempting to contest our seats, and we ask this Convention to give us our seats, as they of right belong to us, and not to cast a stain upon us by raising this man to the dignity of a contest. [Laughter and loud applause.]

We have traveled seven thousand miles to get here. [Applause.] I cannot understand it—though I wish to cast no reflection upon the Executive Committee—but we were detained two days by an accident on the cars, and consequently did not arrive here, and this man has been here two or three days, and has bored this Committee with his credentials—but I cannot understand why the Committee has recognized him in the slightest degree in this contest, unless he, a crawling Copperhead, like the serpent that beguiled Eve, has deceived them with his oily tongue. [Laughter and applause.]

Now, sir, there is no contest in California. One word, and I am done. I simply ask this Convention not to dignify him, or the little squad to which he belongs, and cast a stain upon us by compelling us to go before this Committee on Credentials with a contest, when there is none.

MR. SPENCER, of New York—Mr. Chairman—

MR. NICKERSON, of California—Mr. Chairman—

THE CHAIRMAN—I would suggest to gentlemen, that, when they rise in their seats, they give their names.

MR. NICKERSON, of California—My name is Benjamin R. Nickerson. I wish to ask whether this Convention is prepared to hear, in open Convention, the question which we are prepared to submit where we suppose it belongs—namely, to the Committee on Credentials.

MR. VAN ZANDT, of Rhode Island—Mr Chairman, I again insist on my point of order. Mr. Chairman, I was right in the first place, and this Convention must be aware that (though that entire statement of the gentleman from California may be correct—and, if it be so, my sympathies are intensely and strongly with him, and no man could be more thoroughly so—yet, sir, you will permit me to say—and the gentleman will cherish no feeling of unkindness toward me for saying it, for I believe Rhode Island is as sound to the heart and core on this question as any State in the Union) these are not proper subjects to bring before this Convention. They should go to the Committee on Credentials, because, after one gentleman has told his story, another may rise and claim the attention of the Convention, and tell a story entirely antagonistic to the statement of the first; and how, in the name of parliamentary law, are we to judge between these conflicting claims; or how are we to know which tells the truth? If the statement of the gentleman is correct, my heart is with him entirely; but let the Committee decide the question. I hope my point of order will be sustained by the Convention, for the sake of harmony and unanimity in the Convention, and to enable us to return to our homes in less than a week.

Mr. ———, of California—Mr. Chairman, I rise to a point of order. The State of California has been called, and has named its choice for a member of the Committee on Credentials, and the point of order of the gentleman is too late.

THE CHAIRMAN—The gentleman is out of order. It is moved and seconded that this matter be referred to the Committee on Credentials.

The motion prevailed.

MR. SPENCER, of New York—I move, Mr. Chairman, that the States be called in alphabetical order, that we may ascertain in what States the delegations are contested and in what uncontested, and that a committee of one from each uncontested delegation be named.

THE CHAIRMAN—That is just what we are doing.

The Secretary proceeded to call the States.

MR. ADDAMS, of Illinois—I rise to a point of order. Mr. Chairman, I believe it is the understanding they are to be called in alphabetical order.

THE CHAIRMAN—That is just what we are doing.

MR. ADDAMS, of Illinois—Arkansas, and Alabama, and Georgia have not been called; why are they not called in alphabetical order, harmonizing with the wish of the Convention?

MR. WARD, of New Jersey—Mr. Chairman, I would state that, by the call of the Committee, the unreconstructed States were not invited to be represented here; it being intended that the Convention, when assembled, should decide upon their standing.

MR. ADDAMS, of Illinois—That does not answer my point of order. Mr. Chairman, the point of order I make is that the order of the Convention to call the States in their alphabetical order is not complied with. We would like to know why the names of Arkansas, Alabama, and Georgia have not thus far been called.

MR. SPENCER, of New York—I move that they be called, and we take a vote on each State as it is named.

The motion prevailed.

The Secretary proceeded:

Alabama—J. P. Stow.
Arkansas—S. F. Cooper.
California—P. Conner.

MR. EVANS, of Colorado—Mr. Chairman, as Colorado is only out by the veto of Andrew Johnson, and as he will undoubtedly be out after the Presidental election, I move Colorado be called. [Laughter.]

MR. HALL, of West Virginia—Mr. Chairman, I rise for the purpose of saying a few words to the gentlemen of this Convention preliminary to taking hold of this question, because it involves a point upon which I shall subsequently ask to take the sense of this Convention upon a motion to reconsider. Ever since the close of the war, the Congress of the United States has practically controlled the Southern States as Territories. Upon that basis the whole theory of reconstruction rests.

If it is not correct, then they have been wronged from the first, and Andrew Johnson and the men who have adhered to him have been right in their position. Now, in the case of the State of Colorado, she has not as yet occupied a position, properly, as a State.

MR. SMITHERS, of Delaware—Mr. Chairman, I rise to a question of order. There is no question before the house to which the gentleman is speaking.

THE CHAIRMAN—The motion before the Convention is, that the State of Colorado be called.

MR. HALL, of West Virginia—Mr. Chairman, the question is as to Colorado not being on the roll of States. I hold that she is where she properly belongs as a Territory, until, by Congressional action, full and complete, over the President's veto, her status has been changed. I have no doubt, in the course of time, it will be, but, until that time, she holds, under the Constitution and laws, but one position, and that is as a Territory. There is no half-way place in the making of States. They are admitted or they are not admitted; and, in the case of the Southern States, I voted "aye" with the majority, because I wanted to move to reconsider the vote. I saw it was taken without reflection. The Southern States occupy in the Federal Union to-day, so far as Congressional action is concerned, precisely the position which the State of Colorado occupies. Arkansas is asking admission, and I trust her delegates will be admitted upon this floor. Coming myself from a Border State, I know what the loyal men of the Border States have had to contend with during the last five years; and I shall be the last man, directly or indirectly, to throw the stain of a drop of water, even, upon the character of any man coming from the Border States; and I do not wish this Convention, by its action, seemingly to cast a reflection upon the character of its representatives in Congress during the last three years.

MR. ———, of West Virginia—Mr. Chairman, I wish simply to make the statement that the gentleman's views are his own views, and not the views of the delegation from West Virginia. [Applause.]

MR. SPALDING, of Ohio—Mr. Chairman, if I vote for the admission of Colorado to vote in this Convention, I shall vote for the admission of the three Territories in the same way. They are entitled to seats, but are not voting members. All I ask is, that we treat the Territories all alike. If we vote to receive Colorado, let us vote to receive the others. I am, myself, for the largest liberty.

Mr. McCLURE, of Pennsylvania—Mr. Chairman, there is a difference between Colorado, in this Convention, and any Territory in the United States. Colorado has been authorized by Congress to form a constitution, preparatory to her admission into the Union. She has framed that constitution, and elected her Senators, and applied to Congress for admission. Congress has passed a bill for her admission, and she is only denied it by the force of the matchless traitor of the Union, Andrew Johnson. [Applause.] Colorado has still before the Congress of the United States a bill, which was reported, I believe, before the impeachment. It will doubtless be passed, and at the next election Colorado will be the only Territory that will be likely to vote for President. And, being the only Territory likely so to vote, certainly her case is different to that of any other Territory. I hope, therefore, she will not be put in the position of other Territories, but that she will be admitted into the rights, privileges and powers of this Convention. [Cheers.]

Mr. Spalding, of Ohio—Mr. Chairman, I rise to say, as to the position of Ohio in relation to the admission of delegates from the reconstructed States, that the delegates from Ohio had a consultation upon this subject, and were nearly unanimous in favor of receiving them into the Convention.

Mr. Sharp, of New York—Mr. Chairman, it is the opinion of New York that this Convention is competent to decide upon every case, as it comes up, for itself, and we are in favor of the admission of Colorado over the President's veto. [Applause.]

The Chairman—The question is upon the motion of Mr. Evans, of Colorado, to call the Territory of Colorado in the roll of States.

The motion prevailed.

Mr. Evans, of Colorado—Mr. Chairman, I move that every State and Territory having delegations present be called, and that the delegates therefrom nominate a member to serve on the Committee on Credentials.

Mr. Van Zandt, of Rhode Island—I move that every State and Territory having delegates here representing them, be called, and that it be represented by a member in the Committee on Credentials.

Mr. ———, of ——— —Except Utah. [Laughter. Cries of "No," "no."]

Mr. Van Zandt, of Rhode Island—Very well, I withdraw the motion.

Mr. McClure, of Pennsylvania—Surely, it is not the purpose of the gentleman to do that. Mr. Chairman, I will make a motion that I think will solve the whole problem: That the other Territories of the United States, except Colorado, be admitted to the floor of this Convention, without the right to vote. That was the action of the Convention at Baltimore, in 1864, and I move that the District of Columbia be also excepted.

Mr. Sanders, of Montana—Mr. Chairman, I do think that a journey of three thousand miles through hostile Indians, is considerable to pay for the privilege of sitting here three days in Crosby's Opera-House, and doing nothing. Nobody has a profounder interest in the success of Republican principles than those men that have taken their lives and their convictions in their hands, and have gone to the new empires that are growing in the West. For one, I have come to represent the wishes of, and to give voice to, the thousands of the Republicans of Montana—a people as patriotic, feeling as profound an interest in your action, as any people between the Atlantic and the Pacific. I think the gentleman from Pennsylvania (Mr. McClure) was mistaken in his statement of the action of the Baltimore Convention. I believe it has been uniformly the custom to give those new communities at least one vote in the Convention; and I appeal to the generosity and liberality, if not to the justice, of this Convention, to give us that privilege, and I move to amend the gentleman's resolution by such a proposition as that.

Mr. McClure, of Pennsylvania—I desire simply to repeat, Mr. Chairman, what I can remember most distinctly—that, in 1864, the Territories and a portion of the Southern States were admitted to the floor of the Convention, but not permitted to vote.

Mr. Grout, of Vermont—Let me say, Mr. Chairman, that I am not in the habit of attending Conventions. I don't know what the practice may be. It is announced by the gentleman from Pennsylvania (Mr. McClure) that the practice has never been to give a vote to delegations from Territories. Now, upon principle, I should suppose that would be so—that *would* be so. If it be true—

A VOICE—Mr. Chairman—

THE CHAIRMAN—The gentleman from Vermont (Mr. Grout) has the floor.

MR. GROUT, of Vermont—If it be true, then, Mr. Chairman, we have, in the first place, practice and precedent by which to be guided. We can go back of that, however, if the precedent is wrong, and settle the matter on principle. What is the proposition? The proposition is, to call these Territories—all of them. A gentleman in the rear, somewhere, makes the motion that all the Territories be called that send delegates here. It is impossible for the gentleman calling the roll to know the Territories that have sent delegations. The only way is to call all, and that would include Alaska. [Laughter.] One gentleman proposes to except Utah. Another gentleman might propose to call the roll on the new Territories about to be formed, and the Territory of Wyoming might ask that a delegate be called from that expected Territory. Now it seems to me, though I am but a young man, that this is mere boy's play, the whole of it. ["Louder," "louder."] Mere boy's play, I say. Now, if we call the Territories, and appoint a Committee on Credentials, they have a right to say what representatives shall be admitted from the States. It opens the door, Mr. Chairman, at least, to the right to representation in the nomination of a President and a Vice President. Now, if these Territories have no vote in voting for a President or Vice President, why should they have a vote in nominating them? It seems to me it is opening a wide door, and will only make confusion, and that the only way will be to shut the door against all. The vote has already been taken to admit Colorado into the Convention with the expectation that she shall be admitted as a State. If it is not admitted to cast its vote finally as a State; if it only comes in here and helps to nominate a President and Vice President, but is not admitted to vote at the Presidential election, the Territory of Colorado may have nominated the President of the United States, and not cast even a solitary vote for him. That is wrong. Upon principle, it is wrong. And, if the Convention will attentively consider it, I think they will see it. I say this as but a young man; and I, therefore, want to have some older man, who is used to conventions and their practice, rise and tell us the true way to proceed in this matter. Let them counsel us, and let us proceed deliberately and cautiously in the matter, and in such a manner that, when we go out from this Convention, we shall not regret our course. [Cries of "Mr. Chairman."]

THE CHAIRMAN—The gentleman from Ohio has the floor.

MR. BINGHAM, of Ohio—Mr. Chairman, the Convention has agreed to admit the delegates from those States that we expect will participate in the election of President and Vice President. The Southern States, we expect, will be in the Union, so that their votes will be received and counted. We expect that, notwithstanding Johnson's vetoes, Colorado will be in the Union, so that she can vote. The proposition now is, that the Territories, including the District of Columbia, shall be called, which is a different proposition from the one before. It is not a question whether those Territories will participate in the election. I am not prepared to say how the question will be determined, but it is obvious that we shall save time and proceed in a more orderly manner by leaving the question to the Committee on Credentials, and, therefore, I make that motion.

MR. VAN ZANDT, of Rhode Island—Mr. Chairman, if I am in order, I trust the gentleman will withdraw the motion just made, or modify it. It appears to me that, if this question is referred to the Committee on Credentials, it is an embarrassment which, sir, if the gentleman will withdraw the motion for the admission of this class, will be obviated—by letting the whole question go to the Committee on Credentials. That committee can then report the entire matter to the Convention, with all the facts, and then discussion may understandingly be had upon it at that time.

MR. BINGHAM, of Ohio—That is my motion, exactly.

MR. VAN ZANDT, of Rhode Island—If that is it, and it is so understood by the Convention, I cheerfully second it, and will vote for it.

THE CHAIRMAN—It is moved that the whole matter be referred to the Committee on Credentials.

The motion prevailed.

The Secretary then called the roll, with the following result:

Colorado—John Evans.
Connecticut—W. G. Coe.
Delaware—N. B. Smithers.
Florida—H. H. Moody.
Georgia—L. P. Gudger
Illinois—J. H. Addams.
Indiana—J. C. Albert.
Iowa—E. T. Smith.
Kansas—N. A. Adams.
Kentucky—A. G. Hodges.
Louisiana—A. L. Lee.
Maine—H. M. Plaisted.

Maryland being called—

MR. ———, of Maryland—Mr. Chairman, we have been notified of a contest in half our delegation, and, therefore, we decline to name a delegate upon this committee.

Massachusetts—George B. Loring.
Michigan—John W. Longyear.
Minnesota—John C. Rudolph.
Mississippi—Thadeus B. Sears.
Missouri—David P. Dyer.
Nebraska—L. Girard.
Nevada—Louis Hyntman.
New Hampshire—J. E. Bickford.
New Jersey—John W. Hazelton.
New York—T. G. Younglove.
North Carolina—Hiram Potter, Jr.
Ohio—James Scott.

Oregon—L. S. Thompson.
Pennsylvania—John Cessna.
Rhode Island—J. D. W. Perry.
South Carolina—Henry E. Hayne.
Tennessee—W. Bosson.
Texas—R. K. Smith.
Vermont—Luther Baker.
Virginia—John M. Thacher.
West Virginia—F. P. Pierpont.
Wisconsin—E. L. Browne.

RULES FOR TEMPORARY GOVERNMENT.

MR. COCHRANE, of New York—Mr. Chairman, I move that until the adoption of the permanent rules for the government of this Convention, the rules of the House of Representatives of the United States be the rules for its temporary government, as far as applicable.

The motion prevailed.

COMMITTEE ON PERMANENT ORGANIZATION.

MR. ——, of Pennsylvania—I move, Mr. Chairman, that a committee of one from each State be appointed upon the permanent organization of this Convention.

The motion prevailed.

MR. HALL, of West Virginia—I now move to reconsider the motion by which it was determined to call the roll of the States which are now in process of reconstruction. I would state that the purpose of the motion is, to refer that matter as you have already referred the matter of the Territories—where I think it properly belongs—to the Committee on Credentials. I make the motion with that view, and I trust gentlemen from the Southern States, for whom no man in this house entertains more consideration than I, will not misconstrue this motion.

MR. SPALDING, of Ohio—I rise to a point of order. We have just taken a vote to appoint a Committee on Organization. We should proceed to—

THE CHAIRMAN—I understand the motion of the gentleman from West Virginia to be that the names of the Southern States should not be called. Is not that the motion?

MR. HALL, of West Virginia—The Chairman is somewhat in error. It is to refer the matter to the Committee on Organization—

MR. ———, of Missouri—Mr. Chairman, I rise to a point of order.

Mr. ———, of——— —I move to lay the motion to reconsider on the table, Mr. Chairman.

MR. HALL, of West Virginia—I rise to a question of order, Mr. Chairman. That motion was made while I had the floor.

THE CHAIRMAN—I understand that the gentleman from West Virginia had no longer the floor.

Mr. Hall, of West Virginia—I was asked a question by the Chairman, and had not concluded, when a gentleman from some State rose and made a motion to lay on the table. As I understand it, I had yet the floor.

The Chairman—The motion to lay on the table must not be debated.

Mr. Hall, of West Virginia—As I understand it, the Chairman addressed a question to me and I answered, but I did not give up the floor.

The Chairman—The Chairman decided the gentleman had not the floor

The motion to lay the motion to reconsider on the table prevailed.

The Chairman—The Secretary will call the roll of States, for the names of the Committee on Permanent Organization.

The Secretary proceeded with the call:

Alabama—J. J. Martin.
Arkansas—R. W. McChesney.
California—W. E. Lovett.
Colorado—John Evans.
Connecticut—A. H. Byington.
Delaware—Wilson L. Cannon.
Florida—V. B. Chamberlain.
Georgia—W. H. Watson.
Illinois—Amos C. Babcock.
Indiana—Geo. H. Buskirk.
Iowa—Seth Craig.
Kansas—John A. Martin.
Kentucky—Oscar H. Burbridge.
Louisiana—George C. Benham.
Maine—Wales Hubbard.
Maryland—

Mr. ——, of Maryland—Mr. Chairman, we have two delegations here, and Maryland has no right to be represented on this committee until her delegation is settled by your Committee on Credentials.

Mr. ———, ——— —I move that the name of Maryland be omitted, in the further call of committees, until the report of the Committee on Credentials shall have come in.

The motion prevailed.

The Secretary proceeded with the call:

Massachusetts—Alfred R. Field.
Michigan—Hampton Rich.

The Chairman—I would announce to the Convention that there is a room provided for the Committee on Credentials in the rear of the building, and any member of the Committee of Arrangements will conduct the members of the Committee on Credentials there, now, so that they can go on with the organization.

The Secretary proceeded with the call:

Minnesota—C. C. Andrews.
Mississippi—R. M. Tindall.
Missouri—Geo. A. Moser.
Nebraska—P. B. Stevenson.
Nevada—H. H. Beck.

MR. ———, of ——— —I move that we adjourn for one hour, to wait for the Committee on Credentials.

The motion did not prevail.

MR. ———, of Pennsylvania—Mr. Chairman, it would facilitate business in this Convention if each delegate should hand in the name, and save the calling of the entire delegation from each State; and I move, therefore, that all of these delegations send the name of one delegate for each of these different Committees.

MR. ———, of Michigan—I move as a substitute for that, that, as the names of the several States are called, the Chairman of the delegation announce the name selected by the delegation for the several committees that are to be appointed, so that the roll-call need be gone through with but once.

THE CHAIRMAN—The officers of the Convention are now executing an order of the Convention.

The Secretary proceeded with the call:

New Hampshire—John H. Bailey.
New Jersey—Jarvis H. Bartlett.
New York—Hamilton Harris.
North Carolina—W. R. Myers.
Oregon—R. Mallory.
Ohio—William Stoms.
Pennsylvania—James H. Orne.
Rhode Island—Lysander Flagg.
South Carolina—B. F. Whittemore.
Tennessee—L. C. Houk.
Texas—A. H. Longley.
Vermont—Wm. W. Grout.
Virginia—John Hauxhurst.
West Virginia—E. R. Hall.
Wisconsin—A. Scott Sloan.

THE CHAIRMAN OF THE VIRGINIA DELEGATION—Mr. Chairman—For Virginia, I wish to change, and insert the name of F. M. Kimball.

COMMITTEE ON RESOLUTIONS.

MR. OSBORNE, of Ohio—I offer the following resolution for adoption: In calling the residue of the roll—to save time—I ask, Mr. Chairman, for information whether the present calling is through.

The Chairman—Yes, sir.

Mr. Osborne, of Ohio—Then my motion will come in.

The Secretary read the following resolution, offered by Mr. Osborne, of Ohio:

Resolved, That the several States be called in their order, and that, when so called, the Chairman of the respective delegations declare the names of the Vice President and committeemen as agreed upon by their delegation, and that said names be sent up to the Secretary in writing.

Mr. McClure, of Pennsylvania—I move, Mr. Chairman, as a substitute, or as an amendment—there are but two more committees to appoint—I move, as a substitute for the resolution of the gentleman from Ohio [Mr. Osborne], that this Convention do now proceed to appoint the two committees, as the others have been appointed, but at the same time—one upon resolutions and one upon rules. When the delegations are called, let them give in both at the same time, and then we are through. The committeemen, upon organization, will, of course, know who their States want for Vice President, and will present them in committee. We don't want them presented here. I make that as an amendment or substitute—that we now proceed to appoint the two additional Committees, one upon platform or resolutions and one upon rules, and that the roll be called, and that they both be handed in at the same time—and then we are through.

Mr. Osborne, of Ohio—I have to say to the gentleman of Pennsylvania (Mr. McClure), that it is a mere matter of form. So far as Ohio is concerned, we have selected the man who is to be our Vice President.

Mr. McClure, of Pennsylvania—So have we.

Mr. Osborne, of Ohio—The delegation have agreed upon all these, including the office of President.

Mr. McClure, of Pennsylvania—So have we.

Mr. Osborne, of Ohio—There is no objection, as I see, to sending up the names.

Mr. Lee, of Ohio—Mr. Chairman, I do trust and hope we shall have no more motions and resolutions, but, that this Convention will be quiet, and allow the work to proceed rapidly. [Applause.] I hope this motion and resolution will be voted down, and the calling of the roll will proceed at once. I move to lay the resolution upon the table, although it comes from a colleague.

The motion to lay the resolution on the table prevailed.

The Secretary proceeded to call the roll, and the following Committee on Resolutions was named:

Alabama—Daniel C. Humphreys.
Arkansas—H. B. Morse.
Colorado—Geo. M. Chilcott.
Connecticut—J. M. Woodward.
Delaware—C. S. Layton.

Florida—R. T. Rombeaur.
Georgia—H. K. McCoy.
Illinois—Herman Raster.
Indiana—R. W. Thompson.
Iowa—George M. Dodge.
Kansas—B. F. Simpson.
Kentucky—Charles Eginton.
Louisiana—W. R. Fish.
Maine—Eugene Hale.
Massachusetts—F. W. Bird.
Maryland—John L. Thomas, Jr.
Michigan—Robert R. Beecher.
Minnesota—R. M. McLaren.
Mississippi—A. R. Howe.
Missouri—R. T. Van Horne.
Nebraska—R. W. Furnas.
Nevada—C. E. DeLong.
New Hampshire—James F. Briggs.
New Jersey—John Davidson.
New York—Charles Andrews.
North Carolina—L. G. Estes.
Ohio—John C. Lee.
Oregon—H. R. Kincaid.
Pennsylvania—S. E. Dimmick.
Rhode Island—Rowland G. Hazard.
South Carolina—B. O. Duncan.
Tennessee—William Y. Elliott.
Texas—Geo. W. Paschal.
Vermont—William H. Johnson.
Virginia—Lysander Hill.
West Virginia—Robert S. Brown.
Wisconsin—Horace Rublee.

DISPOSITION OF RESOLUTIONS.

MR. EGINTON, of Kentucky—Mr. Chairman, I offer the following resolution:

Resolved, That all resolutions offered be referred, without debate, to the Committee on Resolutions.

The motion prevailed.

COMMITTEE ON RULES.

Mr. MCCLURE, of Pennsylvania—I ask, now, for the call of the roll, for a Committee on Rules and Order of Business.

THE CHAIRMAN—That will be done unless objections be made.

The Secretary proceeded to call the roll, and the following committee was named:

Alabama—Robert M. Reynolds.
Arkansas—L. H. Roots.
Colorado—J. B. Chaffee.
Connecticut—S. L. Sayles.
Delaware—Isaac J. Jenkins.
Florida—V. B. Chamberlain.
Georgia—David G. Cotting.
Illinois—Emory A. Storrs.
Indiana—G. K. Steele.
Iowa—L. M. Holt.
Kansas—C. W. Babcock.
Kentucky—Thomas J. Pickett.
Louisiana—A. J. Sypher.
Maine—W. P. Harriman.
Maryland—G. W. Z. Black.
Massachusetts—E. Howe.
Michigan—William B. Williams.
Minnesota—A. A. Butler.
Mississippi—D. McA. Williams.
Missouri—A. W. Mullins.
Nebraska—S. A. Strickland.
Nevada—O. R. Leonard.
New Hampshire—E. Vaughan.
New Jersey—C. A. Skillman.
New York—George Barker.
North Carolina—F. F. French.
Ohio—T. L. Young.
Oregon—Maxwell Ramsey.
Pennsylvania—T. E. Cochrane.
Rhode Island—W. H. Reynolds.
South Carolina—J. P. McEpping.
Tennessee—W. J. Smith.
Texas—C. N. Riottet.
Vermont—G. C. Shepard.
Virginia—G. S. Smith.
West Virginia—Henry C. McWhorter.
Wisconsin—A. J. Turner.

THE CHAIRMAN—Your Committee on Permanent Organization having been appointed, what is the further pleasure of the Convention? I would announce to the members of the Committee on Resolutions and on Order of Business, that there are members of the Committee of Arrangements waiting in the hall, to conduct them to their rooms.

MR. SICKLES, of New York—I believe, Mr. Chairman, that all the business which can be accomplished by the temporary organization is disposed of, and I think it is time now we should take a recess, to enable the committees to make their reports.

I, therefore, move that we take a recess until 5 o'clock. [Calls for 4 o'clock.] I would gladly accede to the suggestions made, but, in my judgment, the committees will not be able to report before 5 o'clock, especially the Committee on Credentials. I think I have named the earliest hour.

MR. ———, of ——— —I hope it will be 5 o'clock.

MR. SICKLES, of New York—It will be difficult for the committees to get through before 5 o'clock.

MR. ———, of ——— —I would move that the hour be 7 o'clock, in order to enable the several committees to do their work well.

THE CHAIRMAN—It is moved and seconded that the Convention adjourn until 5 o'clock. To this motion an amendment is offered, that the adjournment be until 7 o'clock.

VOICES—There is no second to the amendment.

THE CHAIRMAN—The motion to adjourn is, that the Convention adjourn until 5 o'clock.

The motion prevailed, and the Convention adjourned.

EVENING SESSION.

The Convention re-assembled, pursuant to adjournment, at 5 o'clock, and was called to order by the Chairman.

CALLS FOR REPORTS.

THE CHAIRMAN—The first business will be the report of the committees, and, unless objection is made, I shall call, first, for the report of the Committee on Permanent Organization. Is the Committee ready to report?

MR. MYERS, of North Carolina—Mr. Chairman, the delegation from North Carolina have been unable to find the Committee, and I desire to hand in the name of Alfred Dochery for Vice-President.

THE CHAIRMAN—The Committee on Permanent Organization will be ready to report in a little while. I have received a series of resolutions passed by the Union League of America, and, unless objected to, I shall refer them to the Committee on Resolutions.

No objection being made, the resolutions were referred to the Committee on Resolutions.

THE CHAIRMAN—The Chairman of the Committee on Permanent Organization is now ready to report.

MR. DAYS, of California—Mr. Chairman, I rise to a point of order. My point of order is, that until the Committee on Credentials report, we do not know who are the members of the Convention, and, hence, we can have no permanent organization.

SEVERAL DELEGATES—"Go on." "Let us hear the report."

MR. CLAFLIN, of Massachusetts—I would suggest that the Committee on Credentials can report all but the contested seats at once, and then we can proceed, and they can report when they get ready. I make that motion, requesting them to report all but the contested seats.

The motion prevailed.

MR. MOREHEAD, of Pennsylvania—Mr. Chairman, while we are waiting for the Committee on Credentials to report, I hope the Committee on Permanent Organization will be permitted to proceed and make their report. I do not think it necessary that the time of the Convention should be delayed. I saw a member of the Committee on Credentials a few minutes ago, a Pennsylvania member, who was going to their committee room. He said they were listening to a long argument from one of the gentlemen from California. I hope the business of the Convention will not be delayed. I move, therefore, that the Committee on Permanent Organization now make their report.

The motion prevailed.

THE CHAIRMAN—The Committee on Permanent Organization will now make their report.

REPORT OF COMMITTEE ON PERMANENT ORGANIZATION.

MR. HAMILTON HARRIS, of New York, Chairman of the Committee on Permanent Organization—Mr. Chairman, I am instructed by the Committee on Permanent Organization to report the name of General Joseph R. Hawley for permanent President of the Convention. [Applause.]

The report was adopted.

THE CHAIRMAN—I would designate Ex-Governor Salomon, of Wisconsin, and Ex-Governor Brown, of Georgia, a committee to conduct Ex-Governor Hawley, of Connecticut, to the chair.

The gentlemen named, then conducted Mr. Hawley to the chair.

Three cheers for Governor Hawley were given.

Three cheers were given for Governor Brown.

Three cheers more were given for the retiring Chairman, General Schurz.

THE CHAIRMAN—Gentlemen, permit me to introduce to you the permanent President of this Convention, Ex-Governor Hawley, of Connecticut.

ADDRESS BY THE PRESIDENT, EX-GOV. HAWLEY, OF CONNECTICUT.

Upon taking the chair, the President said:

GENTLEMEN OF THE CONVENTION: I tender you my most grateful thanks for the high honor you have conferred upon me. Deeply impressed by a sense of the responsibilities of the position, I earnestly solicit your indulgence and your aid. We come together, charged with the momentous duty of selecting the chief rulers of the great nation which leads the world in the promotion of freedom and equal rights. [Applause.] The indications of your purpose and spirit already given, assure us that you will maintain the noble character of the Republican party.

We unavoidably recall the Convention of 1860, with its profound anxieties, its fresh, pure and glowing devotion to liberty, and its enthusiastic acceptance of the wager of battle tendered by slavery and secession. [Applause.] It now seems to clear to us that God ruled our councils. [Great applause.] He made our declaration of principles manly and sincere. He gave us Abraham Lincoln for President. [Tremendous cheering.] May He send us like wisdom and success to-day. [Applause.]

He tested us in a manner, and to an extent, which the liveliest imagination could not have anticipated. Posterity, we hope, will decide that we met that test with the spirit worthy of a free people. Countless treasure, and three hundred thousand lives freely offered, are the evidences that we were solemnly in earnest. We offered our lives and our property; but it was not enough. We laid our prejudices of race and class upon the altar, and the consciousness that we at last deserved success redoubled our strength. The same high resolve rules to-day, and the Union men of this country are ready for equal and even greater sacrifices, if they be indispensable to the dedication of this Continent to liberty and equal rights. [Applause.]

We learned the first lesson when we found that we must make all men free, and call all men to the battle-field. We learned the second lesson when we found that we must still move on and give impartially to all men a share in the Government we were endeavoring to restore. [Great applause.]

With a clear and fearless expression of the essential and important questions at issue—which the people well understand, and no ingenious device, no words can obscure or avoid—passing by all personal and temporary controversies, working in perfect confidence that the American people mean to do right, and will do it in the end, we may feel sure of triumph. The power of a nation of forty millions must be behind the just claim of the poorest workingman, of whatever race, to recover even and just wages. Its majesty must be felt wherever the humblest loyal man appeals against personal violence and oppression. [Cheers.] For every dollar of the national debt, the blood of a soldier is pledged. [Great cheering.] Every bond, in letter and in spirit, must be as sacred as a soldier's grave. [Cheers.] We must win, gentlemen, and we *shall* win. It is the old fight of liberty, equality and fraternity, against oppression, caste and aristocracy. It is the old fight to make the world better, with "malice toward none, and charity for all." [Loud applause.]

We may halt for a moment, or change direction, but the good cause always goes steadily forward. It is related—and, whether it be true or not, the incident is well invented—that, on the evening of that awful battle of the Wilderness, when the legions of the Union army had fought all day, rather by faith than by sight, in the wild woods and tangled brush, that some one asked General Grant to step backward a little, and re-organize, and that he replied, "We have done very well, gentlemen! At half past three in the morning we move *forward!*" [Long and continued cheering.] We accept his spirit and his words.

Perhaps I am not anticipating in saying that we shall accept him in person again as our leader. [Loud cheering.]

Thanking you again, gentlemen, very heartily for the honor conferred, I await the pleasure of the Convention. [Applause.]

FURTHER REPORT OF COMMITTEE ON PERMANENT ORGANIZATION.

MR. HAMILTON HARRIS, of New York, Chairman of the Committee on Permanent Organization, then further reported, as follows:

FOR PRESIDENT.

GENERAL JOSEPH R. HAWLEY, OF CONNECTICUT.

FOR VICE PRESIDENTS.

Alabama—Willard Warner.
Arkansas—A. McDonald.
California—James Coey.
Colorado—J. B. Chaffee.
Connecticut—W. H. Pierson.
Delaware—Lewis Thompson.
Florida—H. H. Moody.
Georgia—Foster Blodgett.
Illinois—Jesse K. Dubois.
Indiana—W. Q. Gresham.
Iowa—J. M. Hedrick.
Kansas—S. S. Prouty.
Kentucky—J. F. Speed.
Louisiana—W. P. Kellogg.
Maine—T. A. D. Fessenden.
Maryland—Henry Stockbridge.
Massachusetts—D. W. Gooch.
Michigan—Henry Waldron.
Minnesota—Horatio P. Van Cleve.
Mississippi—Thos. L. White.
Missouri—A. J. Harlan.
Montana—W. F. Sanders.
Nebraska—A. Saunders.
Nevada—J. M. Walker.
New Hampshire—E. Gould.

New Jersey—Jno. S. Irick.
New York—Chauncey M. Depew.
North Carolina—Alfred Dockery.
Ohio—N. C. McFarland.
Oregon—J. R. Failing.
Pennsylvania—J. K. Morehead.
Rhode Island—W. Green.
South Carolina—Carlos T. Stolbrand.
Tennessee—T. A. Hamilton.
Texas—S. D. Wood.
Vermont—G. J. Stannard.
Virginia—J. Burke.
West Virginia—S. D. Karns.
Wisconsin—Edward Salomon.

SECRETARIES.

Thomas D. Fister,
V. Dell,
C. B. Higby,
F. B. Salomon,
B. Bent,
Joshua T. Heald,
J. Rhombeaur,
Geo. G. Wilber,
James P. Root,
Chas. R. Hogate,
J. H. Easton,
Lewis Weil,
Charles Seymour,
Wm. C. Goodloe,
C. W. Lowell,
Stephen D. Lindsey,
E. F. Waters,
Geo. G. Briggs,
W. W. Scott,
A. Worley Patterson,
J. C. S. Colby,
Samuel Maxwell,
G. N. Collins,
Francis B. Ayer,
Robt. C. Bellville,
Luther Caldwell,
J. W. Holden,
Coates Kenney,
Max Ramsey,
A. C. Harmer,
—— Pehiter,
Wm. E. Rose,
T. McKinley,
Wm. P. Home,
S. D. Ringree,
Edgar Allen.
Joseph T. Hoke.

MR. ———, of New York—Before we vote on the adoption of the report, I ask the members from the State of Maine the name of their Vice President.

MR. SHEPLEY, of Maine—T. A. D. Fessenden.

Upon motion, the report of the Committee on Permanent Organization was adopted.

MR. ———, of Illinois—I have a suggestion to make: That when a member rises to address the Chair, he immediately announce the State from which he comes. This would save a great deal of confusion, and enable the Chair to recognize the person.

THE PRESIDENT—I will suggest that they add their own name in case of any extended remarks—at least, give their names and their State.

MOTION TO NOMINATE.

Mr. Swift, of Indiana—Mr. President, as the first and most fitting act of this Convention, after the permanent organization, I move, now, that General Ulysses S. Grant be declared its nominee for President by acclamation. [Cries of "No," "no." "Too early."]

DELEGATION FROM THE SOLDIERS' AND SAILORS' CONVENTION.

Mr. Cochrane, of New York—Mr. President, I am informed that there is a committee in waiting from the Soldiers' and Sailor's Convention, which convened and finished their proceedings on yesterday, charged with the duties of presenting those proceedings to this Convention. I move you, sir, a committee of five be appointed to escort them into the presence of this Convention, so that they may hereupon and now discharge their duties.

The motion prevailed.

Mr. Cowles, of North Carolina—I move now, sir, that the Vice Presidents take their seats upon the stand, in order to put the platform in shape for the reception of the delegation.

The President—Gentlemen, you have heard the suggestion. So far as it is possible, it will be well that the Vice Presidents and Secretaries should take their seats upon the stage. [Laughter.]

Mr. Bartholomew, of Pennsylvania—Mr. President, as the business of the Convention will necessarily be delayed a few moments, preparatory to the reception of this committee, and the report of committees now appointed and in action, I move you, sir, that General Daniel E. Sickles be invited to address this Convention on the topics of the day. [Cheers. "Good," "good."]

Mr. Sickles, of New York—Mr. President, I beg the gentleman to withdraw that request. I should be very happy, on some proper occasion, to address this body, but at this time I should be very reluctant to interrupt the process of business with any remarks. Besides, I am one of the delegation to this body from the Soldiers' and Sailors' Convention, and my duties will require me, in a very few minutes, to join that deputation to present the proceedings of the Soldiers' and Sailors' Convention to this body.

Mr. Bartholomew, of Pennsylvania—Under the explanation, I withdraw my motion.

The President—The Chair announces as the Committee to receive the delegation from the Soldiers' and Sailors' Convention: Gen. Cochrane, of New York; Gen. Schurz, of Missouri; Gen. Dodge, of Iowa; Gen. Sweet, of Illinois.

Mr. ——, of —— —Mr. Dodge, of Iowa, is on the Committee on Resolutions, and is absent from the building. I would suggest the name of Col. Craig in place of Gen. Dodge.

The President—The name of Col. Craig will be taken in place of Gen. Dodge, if there is no objection.

The delegation of the Soldiers' and Sailors' Convention was conducted to the front of the platform.

MR. COCHRANE, of New York—Mr. President, I have the honor, in behalf of the committee recently appointed by yourself, to announce that they have discharged the duty to which they were appointed. I introduce to the Convention, through yourself, Gen. Fairchild, of Wisconsin, Chairman of the Committee from the Soldiers' and Sailors' Convention. [Prolonged applause.]

GEN. FAIRCHILD, of Wisconsin—Mr. President and gentlemen of the Convention—As instructed by the members of the Soldiers' and Sailors' Convention, I appear before you in their behalf, to present to you a resolution, passed unanimously by them yesterday afternoon, as follows:

"*Resolved*, That we, the soldiers and sailors, steadfast now, as ever, to the Union and the flag, fully recognize the claims of General Ulysses S. Grant to the confidence of the American people, and believing that the victories won under his guidance in war will be illustrated by him in peace, by such measures as will secure the fruits of our exertions, and restore the Union upon the loyal basis, we declare it as our deliberate conviction that he is the choice of the soldiers and sailors of the Union for the office of President of the United States of America." [Loud applause.]

Mr. President and gentlemen—The soldiers of the United States ask the nomination of General Grant for President of the United States, because we love him; and we love him, sir, because he is loyal to the Union, loyal to justice, loyal to freedom, and loyal to right; and if you will give us our comrade as leader in the campaign of 1868, we will bear down upon the enemy's works as we did upon the enemy's works in the field in 1864. [Applause.]

THE PRESIDENT—It is hardly necessary that I should say that such a communication is received with the warmest interest from Republican Soldiers and Sailors by a Republican Convention. The communication is before you.

MR. SPALDING, of Ohio—I propose three cheers for the soldiers and sailors.

Three hearty cheers were given.

MOTION TO NOMINATE—AGAIN.

MR. LANE, of Indiana—Mr. President, I move you that the nomination of General Ulysses S. Grant be now declared by acclamation by this Convention. [Cries—"Wait awhile." "The Committee on Credentials hasn't reported." "Question."]

THE PRESIDENT—The motion as made is seconded.

MR. TREMAIN, of New York—Mr. President, I presume there is no member of this Convention who is not prepared at the proper time to indorse the recommendation made by the soldiers and sailors. I presume there is not one loyal heart that does not beat in unison with the sentiment that calls upon us to select that great chieftain, Ulysses S. Grant, as our standard-bearer in this campaign. [Applause.] Sir, I want the proceedings of this Convention to go forth with such dignity, and as the result of such deliberation as not only will command our approval, but the approval of those who sent us here. [Applause.]

Now, I happened to be present at the Convention in Baltimore, in 1864, when the same unanimity prevailed that called upon the representatives of the people to select Abraham Lincoln as their standard-bearer. [Applause.] But, sir, a motion to nominate him by acclamation was superseded by a motion that the States should be called in their order, and that, as each State was called, from its response we should have the moral force arising from the unanimous expression of each one of the delegates from that State. [Applause.] Sir, when that is done, the Convention will be at liberty, by acclamation, to second the nomination, as the people will—not only in their preliminary meetings, but at the polls. [Applause.]

I hope, therefore, my friend from Indiana, [Mr. Lane,] will withdraw the motion, until the States can be called in their order.

MR. LANE, of Indiana—Mr. President, I certainly have no desire to consume the time of the Convention. I only wish to get at the object. The nomination is already made, sanctioned by the people, and by the whole people. But, if it is thought better to call the States—call the States! [Laughter.] Call the States! [Laughter and applause.]

MR. BEACH, of Ohio—I would remark, in this connection, that we are not organized. The Committee on Credentials have not yet reported the delegates who are entitled to seats here, and to do anything of this kind in an unorganized condition is not appropriate.

MR. LOGAN, of Illinois—[Applause and cheers]—Mr. President, I desire merely to remark, that I think it would be a more appropriate mode of proceeding to accept the report of the committee from the Soldiers' and Sailors' Convention; that, then, when this Convention will be fully organized, and when the States are represented by their delegates who shall have been accepted by the Convention, after the report of the Committee on Credentials, then the order of business would be nomination of candidates for President. [Applause.]

I know, sir, that General Grant, of whom we are all proud, from one end of this broad land to the other, is, to-day, the nominee of the loyal citizens, the loyal soldiers and the loyal sailors of this grand and glorious country. And I simply desire to make this suggestion, that the Convention may consider it. As far as the making of the nomination by a delegate from any particular State is concerned, we, Illinoisans, have no pride whatever. We had as lief the nomination would come from one State as another, and I merely make these remarks with reference to the mode and order of proceeding. [Applause.]

MR. COCHRANE, of New York—Mr. President, I move you, sir, as an amendment to the resolution which has been offered, and, if that resolution is withdrawn, then as an independent resolution, that the resolutions from the Soldiers' and Sailors' Convention, as reported, be accepted by the Convention, entered upon its record, and made a part of its proceedings.

MR. LANE, of Indiana—I will withdraw for that purpose.

The motion prevailed.

CALL FOR THE COMMITTEE ON CREDENTIALS.

MR. PIERCE, of Virginia—Mr. President, I would now call, sir, for the report of the Committee on Credentials, that we may know who there are here—whether we have a convention or a mass-meeting. I would move you, sir, that the Committee on Credentials be called upon now to make a report regarding all the states where there is no contest.

THE PRESIDENT—I am informed that a motion to that effect has already been adopted. It was postponed for a time, waiting for the report of the Committee on Permanent Organization. Is there any member of the Committee on Credentials who can inform us whether that committee is ready, or even partly so?

MR. ———, of ——— —I desire to inform the Convention that it is not yet ready to report. It has a contested case before it, which is not yet determined, and probably will not be for an hour.

THE PRESIDENT—It seems to be the desire of the Convention to hear a report from the committee, as far as possible. If there be but one State remaining, the Convention wishes, as far as I can judge its sentiments, to hear from the rest. [Cries of "Logan," "Logan."]

MR. LOGAN, of Illinois—I beg, gentlemen, that you will excuse me. I do not wish to take up the time of the Convention now. At an appropriate time I have, certainly, no objection to respond, but at present I would rather not delay the Convention. [Cries of "Committee," "Committee."]

THE PRESIDENT—The Chairman would inform the Convention that it has twice sent word to the committee in question, and that it is expected every moment. [Cries of "Committee."] The Chairman sends word that they have finished all the contested cases, and will be here in five minutes, or as soon as they can prepare their report. [Laughter.]

MR. CONWAY, of Louisiana—Mr. President, I suppose that it is a part of the settled policy of the Republican party, to-day, to have the South come into this Convention Union end foremost. [Applause and laughter.] But we have another marked event, of special moment—that there is with us to-day, in full heart and in full fellowship, one of the former Governors, in the days of the rebellion, of one of the rebellious States, who has since become reconstructed [applause], has proved himself, in the fire, as true as steel, a genuine convert, and in fellowship with the Republican party.

I move, sir, that during the interim, until we have the report of the Committee on Credentials, Ex-Governor Joseph E. Brown, of Georgia, be invited to address the Convention. [Applause. Cries of "Brown," "Brown."]

THE PRESIDENT—It is hardly necessary to put a motion which has such a reception. Will Governor Brown address the Convention?

MR. BROWN, of Georgia—Mr. President, as it has been announced that the committee will be ready to report in a few minutes, I think it might be improper that I should attempt to enter into any discussion of the questions involved at this time. And I could not do justice to myself or my section if I attempted to speak without time to review, to some extent, the questions involved.

I do not wish, sir, to intrude upon the proceedings of this Convention. I came here, as has been well remarked, a reconstructed rebel. [Laughter and applause.] I was an original secessionist. [Laughter. Cries of "That's frank." "An open confession is good for the soul." Cries of "Platform," amid which Mr. Brown advanced to the stage.]

THE PRESIDENT—Gov. Brown, of Georgia, gentlemen. [Tremendous applause.]

MR. BROWN, of Georgia—Mr. President and gentlemen of the Convention.

A VOICE—"Tell us your experience." Laughter and applause.

MR. BROWN, of Georgia—As I remarked before I left my seat, I was an original secessionist. I was born in the State of South Carolina, in Mr. Calhoun's district. [Laughter.] Charmed with the fascination of his manner and the splendor of his intellect, I early imbibed his State Rights doctrines, and I suppose that I religiously believed that they were correct, as you believed that your doctrines were correct. I believe that I had seen for ten years, before the unfortunate struggle we have just passed through, that the issues which divided the North and South must ultimately be settled by the sword. There was no common tribunal whose judgment we would respect. If the Supreme Court decided a question bearing upon the great issues, the party against whom the decision was made refused to abide by it, because it was regarded as political. And, while I deprecated the necessity, I believed one day it must come. While Mr. Clay lived—that great man—that great pacificator—[cheers and great applause]—we were able to avert this issue. But Mr. Clay was called from his field of usefulness, and Mr. Webster died, and Mr. Calhoun slept with his fathers; and when the storm again rose there was no one who could pour oil upon the troubled waters and stop the deluge. Secession was the result! I went into it cordially, as a States' Rights man, and I stood by it—[cheers]—as long as there was any chance to sustain it. When the President of the Confederate States abandoned the great States' Rights doctrine that we commenced the revolution upon, I differed from him. When he adopted his conscript measures, which gave the entire control of the whole army of the Confederate States to the President, with the appointment of every officer, down to the lowest Lieutenant—an error, sir, that your Government did not make—I took issue with him. But we went through the struggle. I will not attempt now to review its history, but we of the South fell, and you of the great North were the conquerors; and I think I had sense enough at the end of the struggle to know when I was whipped. [Cheers.]

The President of the United States, after the surrender of Gen. Johnston, ordered my arrest and imprisonment. After my release your courts were open and I was left free to act. I felt then that the time had come when I should make my choice between this land and this Government, and some other land and some other Government. I still love my own native land the best. [Cheers, and cries of "Good," "good."] And, with your construction of the Constitution, established by the sword, I still preferred the Government of the United States to any other recognized Government. [Cheers.]

The natural inquiry then was: What is my interest, and what is my duty? I believed it was my interest, and my choice, to remain in this Government. If I remained here, I must seek the amnesty of the Government for the past, and I must seek its protection for the future. If it yielded me that, I was in honor bound to return to my allegiance and make a good citizen, if I could. [Cries of "Good," "good," and cheers.] Hence, I have advocated every measure from that time until this, for reconstruction. [Applause.] When the President of the United States proposed his plan, I advised our people to accept it; because we had fallen, and we had no other power to negotiate with but him. He did not call Congress together.

When Congress, which had the legitimate control of this question—[cheers and prolonged applause], proposed the Constitutional Amendment to the Southern States, I advised such friends as sought my opinion upon the question, that it was better to accept it. But the feeling was so overwhelming against it that no voice could stay it. Unwisely, the Southern States promptly rejected those terms. I did not then suppose it would ever get better terms. I was satisfied we must submit to worse ones. What was that Constitutional Amendment?

There was but one living issue in it, and that was the suffrage question—and that Congress left with the States to settle for themselves. If we voted the black race, we must count them in our representation; if we refused to vote them we could not count them. That was right! [Cheers and great applause. Cries of "Right! right!"]

With reference to the Federal debt, there was no question there.

There was but one other important measure connected with it; that was the provision that disqualified me, and others in my condition, from holding office. That was no living issue. I and others like me will soon pass from the stage, and if we are never relieved by Congress there are other and better men to take our places. Therefore, in my judgment, we acted unwisely.

What next followed? The Supplemental Bill and the Sherman Act. I advised, immediately on the passage of that act, that we promptly accept the terms. At that time it would have been easy for me. True, without vanity, I may say I had some popularity in my State, and had four times been elected the Executive of my State. I might have retained and courted popularity. But duty and my judgment dictated to me a different course. I did it; and I have received the hearty denunciation of my people—or a large proportion of them—for having done so.

I have been denounced as a traitor to my race, and a traitor to the "*Lost Cause*" which I had so much at heart. I do not think so. I think my course more honorable than the course of that man who was a rebel and sought the same amnesty that I sought, and received the same protection from the Government that I received, and then stays in its bosom its enemy, prepared to sting it when opportunity offers. ["Good," "good," and Applause.] When I fought you, I fought you openly and boldly. When I surrendered, I surrendered in good faith. [Cheers.] And when I took the amnesty oath, I took it with a purpose religiously to observe it. By my theory (and I had been taught that it is the true one), my primary allegiance was to the State. When I had formally taken an oath to support the Constitution of the United States, I understood it to bind me only while my State remained in the Union; but if she withdrew (which I believed she had the right to do, for just cause, by the very necessity of the case), I thought she must be the judge. I did not feel that I had violated that oath when I went with my State. But, since that time, when the President of the United States offered me his pardon, he required me to take a very different oath. I was sworn to support not only the Constitution of the United States, but the Union of the States. [Applause.] When I did that I abandoned the doctrine of secession, for I cannot support the union of the States and encourage secession from the Union. [Cheers.] The Virginia and Kentucky resolutions that included that doctrine, as I understood them, had always been the very platform upon which the Democracy had stood. But when the platform was knocked from under my party, I had nothing left to take hold on. As I understood the doctrines of the Democratic party, they were sovereignty and the right of secession. The sword has established a different doctrine, and hence it is that I am no longer bound by party allegiance to stand by the Democratic party. Where do I naturally fall, then? The Hamiltonian and Websterian construction of the Constitution has been established by the sword. I have acquiesced in that, and, as I find the Republican party on that platform to-day, my oath has bound me to abandon the doctrine which the Democratic party stood upon, and that naturally leads me, as I think, into the Republican party. [Cheers.] I know this is a very unpopular doctrine in the South, but I believe it is the true doctrine. But let me tell you, Mr. President and gentlemen, that there are many white men in the South, there are large numbers of original Democrats in the South, there are large numbers of orginal secessionists in the South, who, to-day, stand as firmly by the Republican party, and will support the great Captain of the age, Gen. Grant—[great applause]—as well as you will.

Our Democratic friends have appealed to the whole country against negro suffrage, have showered anathemas upon it, and denounced it as an outrage upon humanity and upon society; and yet, in the late elections there, the negro who would vote the Democratic ticket was really a very respectable fellow!—[laughter]—while a white man who voted the Republican ticket was a scalawag and a traitor! [Cheers and laughter.] They tell us: then you establish negro supremacy in the South. Not so; not so. Although they denounce those of us who act with the Republican party as being no better than negroes, I still feel I belong to the white race, and that I would advocate and sustain no policy that put any other race over my race in the South, or made them supreme there. While we grant to the colored people all their rights, civil and political, we do not expect them to be our masters. Much as you have seen in the papers on that subject, it is not so. In the State of Georgia, for instance, when those who are included in the constitutional amendment, and who will be voters, although they have no right to hold offices under our new constitution, come to the ballot-box, there are twenty thousand majority of white men there. What little property is left, is all in the hands of the white men. We have the advantage of education. We have the advantage in experience, and we claim that we have superiority of race. Tell me not, then, that the black people of Georgia can rule Georgia, when they are twenty thousand in the minority, and we have all these advantages. This is said with a view of prejudicing the Republican party, North and South. Is it not so? In other States, even where the blacks are in the majority, if our white race act properly in this matter, there will be no difficulty of that sort.

I am aware I am taking up too much time. [Cries—"Go on."]

THE PRESIDENT—Is the Chairman of the Committee here?

MR. BROWN, of Georgia—I will thank you, at any moment, to interrupt me when the committee comes in. [A voice—"It is coming now."]

MR. BROWN, of Georgia—Just in conclusion, let me say, while we have a hard fight to make in Georgia, if you will give us the fruits of the victory we have lately won in a desperate fight, we will carry Georgia for General Grant. [Great applause.]

Allow me one word before I take my seat. I have said, if we do it, you must give us the fruits of our victory. We have elected our Governor; we have adopted our Constitution by a large majority, and we have elected a majority in both branches of the General Assembly. Yet our Governor is not inaugurated, our Legislature is not called together. We desire that Mr. Stevens' bill, that passed the House of Representatives the other day, be slightly amended in the Senate, and there passed. Then we are on our feet. And the amendment we desire is this: That the Senate of the United States amend that bill so as to allow the Governor elect—Governor Bullock—to convene his Legislature on ten days' notice; let him be inaugurated, let them act, and they will adopt the constitutional amendment; and then let them elect Senators, and receive us into Congress, and give us control of the State Government and its patronage, which we fought for and won, and which we must have if we are to succeed in this contest. [Great applause.]

REPORT OF THE COMMITTEE ON CREDENTIALS.

MR. LEE, of Louisiana, Chairman of the Committee on Credentials—Mr. President, your committee report the names of the several delegates from the several States, and especially report in reference to the State of Pennsylvania, that there appeared fifty-nine delegates, whereas that State is entitled, under the call, to only fifty-two votes in this Convention; that your committee recommend that those fifty-nine delegates named in their report be admitted to seats upon the floor of the Convention, and that they be authorized to cast the fifty-two votes to which the State is entitled, such being the wish of the Pennsylvania delegation.

Your committee have further reported in favor of allowing to each of the delegations from the several Territories, and, also, the District of Columbia, the right to seats upon the floor, and the privilege of casting, each, two votes. And, further, Mr. President, we report to you the names of delegates from the States of Maryland and California, which, in our judgment, are entitled to seats upon the floor, and to a voice in the Convention.

MR. ———, of ——— —I move, now, that the delegates reported from California and Maryland be read by the Secretary.

MR. WARNER, of Alabama—I ask for information whether the delegates from the unreconstructed States are included in this report?

MR. LEE, of Louisiana—I would state that the delegates from the unreconstructed States are included in this report as entitled to seats and votes. [Applause.] I will state that the committee considered that the action of the Convention, this morning, effectually settled that question.

MR. ———, of Maryland—Before the names of the delegates from those two States are read, I desire to ask my friend, the Chairman of the Committee, to make this statement in regard to the delegation from Maryland: The committee resolved that the delegation headed by Mr. Cresswell should be admitted to seats on the floor with the right to cast votes, and that the delegation headed by Ex-Governor Thomas and Judge Bond, should be admitted to the floor with the right to have seats thereon, without being permitted to vote.

MR. LEE, of Louisiana—That is correct.

THE PRESIDENT—The report will be filed by the Secretary.

LIST OF DELEGATES.

ALABAMA.

	Delegates.	Alternates.	
At Large—	Robert M. Reynolds	——	——
	David C. Humphreys	——	——
	James P. Stow	——	——
	Thomas D. Fister	——	——
Dist. 1—	Albert Griffin	——	——
	Almon M. Granger	——	——
2—	Willard Warner	——	——
	John C. Keffer	——	——
3—	John J. Martin	——	——
	Robert T. Smith	——	——
4—	Thomas L. Tullock	——	——
	Benjamin S. Williams	——	——
5—	William J. Haralson	——	——
	Joseph W. Burke	——	——
6—	G. M. Tabor	——	——
	Jacob Y. Cantwell	——	——

ARKANSAS.

	Delegates.	Alternates.	
At Large—	Benjamin F. Rice	——	——
	Alexander McDonald	——	——
	W. H. Gray	——	——
	R. W. McChesney	——	——
Dist. 1—	W. S. McCullough	——	——
	W. H. Rogers	——	——
2—	H. B. Morse	——	——
	L. H. Roots	——	——
3—	Samuel F. Cooper	——	——
	Valentine Dill	——	——

CALIFORNIA.

	DELEGATES.	ALTERNATES.
AT LARGE—	James Coey	—— ——
	P. E. Conner	—— ——
	J. Stratman	—— ——
DIST. 1—	Wm. H. Sears	—— ——
	Wm. E. Lovett	—— ——
2—	C. B. Higby	—— ——
	J. M. Days	—— ——
3—	Thomas Spencer	—— ——
	J. S. Rogers	—— ——

COLORADO.

AT LARGE—	John Evans	—— ——
	Jerome B. Chaffee	—— ——
	Geo. M. Chilcott	—— ——
	Harper M. Orahood	—— ——
	John C. Anderson	—— ——
	James Peck	—— ——

CONNECTICUT.

AT LARGE—	J. R. Hawley	—— ——
	O. H. Platt	—— ——
	Marshall Jewell	—— ——
	Thomas Clark	—— ——
DIST. 1—	H. W. Carr	W. S. Pierson
	E. M. Smith	Patten Fitch
2—	S. W. Kellogg	James M. Woodward
	Bartlett Bent, Jr	Thomas Clark
3—	Horace Smith	—— ——
	Sabin L. Sayles	—— ——
4—	Wm. G. Coe	Truman A. Warren
	A. Homer Byington	—— ——

DAKOTA.

DELEGATES.	ALTERNATES.
G. C. Moody	J. L. Jolley
C. B. Valentine	J. R. Hanson

DELAWARE.

Joshua T. Heald	James B. Henry
Nathaniel B. Smithers	Wilson L. Cannon
Caleb S. Layton	S. D. Strawbridge
Lewis Thompson	John F. Williamson
Thomas B. Coursey	Jas. R. Lofland
Isaac J. Jenkins	George Joseph

DISTRICT OF COLUMBIA.

Sayles J. Bowen	——— ———
Wm. L. Morse	——— ———
G. W. Wells	——— ———
Benjamin N. Meeds	——— ———
Samuel L. Brown	——— ———

FLORIDA.

H. H. Moody	——— ———
S. B. Connover	——— ———
R. T. Rombeaur	——— ———
V. B. Chamberlin	——— ———

GEORGIA.

	DELEGATES.	ALTERNATES.	
At Large—	Foster Blodgett	——	——
	Joseph E. Brown	——	——
	J. R. Parrott	——	——
	H. K. McCoy	——	——
Dist. 1—	T. P. Robb	——	——
	Isaac Seeley	——	——
2—	F. O. Welch	——	——
	D. B. Harrell	——	——
3—	I. G. Maull	——	——
	W. C. Smith	——	——
4—	G. G. Wilbur	——	——
	J. B. Etze	——	——
5—	D. G. Cotting	——	——
	Wm. Gibson	——	——
6—	Madison Bell	——	——
	E. Hulbert	——	——
7—	L. P. Gudger	——	——
	W. H. Watson	——	——

IDAHO.

J. H. Alvord	——	——
Geo. I. Gilvert	——	——

ILLINOIS.

	DELEGATES.	ALTERNATES.
AT LARGE—	John A. Logan	J. D. Galloway
	A. C. Babcock	T. W. Harris
	John H. Addams	E. S. Conditt
	B. J. Sweet	W. D. Henderson
	Jesse K. Dubois	C. H. Ray
	Emory A. Storrs	D. G. Hays
DIST. 1—	J. Russel Jones	Merrill Ladd
	Herman Raster	L. P. Otis
2—	M. L. Joslyn	Chauncey Ellwood
	Wm. Hulin	Robert Swain
3—	James L. Camp	R. V. Aukney
	M. D. Swift	C. B. Smith
4—	Calvin Truesdale	K. K. Jones
	Ira D. Chamberlain	H. W. Draper
5—	W. L. Wiley	P. M. Blair
	Mark Bangs	J. S. Merrier
6—	Henry Fish	W. H. Palmerston
	Calhoun Grant	W. C. Goodhue
7—	J. W. Langley	A. B. Reff
	James Steele	Thomas Apperson
8—	Giles A. Smith	John McWilliams
	J. S. Whittinger	Henry S. Green
9—	G. W. Whitney	L. S. Allard
	Hugh N. Fullerton	B. R. Hangton
10—	John Logan	George L. Zine
	A. C. Vandeventer	David Pierson
11—	J. A. Powell	A. B. Barrett
	W. O. Robinson	W. H. Blakely
12—	T. E. Hosmer	John McCutchins
	Philip Eisenmyer	W. H. Copp
13—	B. G. Root	J. C. Willis
	Thos. S. Ridgeway	W. A. Sweeney

INDIANA.

	DELEGATES.	ALTERNATES.
At Large—	Robert W. Thompson	D. C. Branham
	Henry S. Lane	Silas Colgrove
	William A. Peele	Daniel D. Pratt
	Walter Q. Gresham	John W. Foster
Dist. 1—	Cyrus M. Allen	Dr. A. Lewis
	Lemuel Q. DeBruler	D. C. Jacquess
2—	Andrew Caskin	John F. Carr
	John C. Albert	J. B. Merriwether
3—	John G. Berkshire	Smith Vawter
	A. W. Prather	D. G. Rabb
4—	Kichard H. Swift	Joseph Livingston
	Benj. F. Claypool	Nimrod H. Johnson
5—	Chas. F. Hogate	Ezra Olleman
	Wm. M. French	G. H. Voss
6—	George K. Steele	John P. Baird
	Geo. H. Buskirk	Harrison Woodsmall
7—	Joseph Odell	W. J. Templeton
	James H. Paris	Robert Fisher
8—	John Brownlee	John Green
	J. D. Conner	Daniel H. Bennett
9—	S. T. Powell	H. H. Neff
	John H. Hough	Jacob M. Haines
10—	S. P. Williams	D. D. Dickenson
	J. W. Purviance	O. H. Woodworth
11—	Aaron Gurney	Oliver H. P. Bailey
	C. G. Powell	W. H. Butterworth

IOWA.

	DELEGATES.	ALTERNATES.	
AT LARGE—	Peter Melendy	——	——
	G. M. Dodge	——	——
	J. A. Williamson	——	——
	J. M. Hedrick	——	——
DIST. 1—	Seth Craig	——	——
	Joshua Tracy	——	——
2—	J. C. Polley	——	——
	J. McKean	——	——
3—	A. J. Felt	——	——
	J. H. Easton	——	——
4—	N. B. Vinyard	——	——
	A. J. Pope	——	——
5—	E. H. Sears	——	——
	E. T. Smith	——	——
7—	R. A. Smith	——	——
	L. M. Holt	——	——

KANSAS.

C. W. Babcock	——	——
Benjamin F. Simpson	——	——
John A. Martin	——	——
S. S Prouty	——	——
N. A. Adams	——	——
Louis Weil	——	——

KENTUCKY.

	DELEGATES.	ALTERNATES.	
AT LARGE—	Joshua F. Speed	——	——
	Geo. T. Wood	——	——
	Charles Eginton	——	——
	A. G. Hodges	——	——
DIST. 1—	Samuel L. Casy	——	——
	Thomas J. Pickett	——	——
2—	O. P. Johnson	——	——
	Walter Evans	——	——
3—	Thomas Crutcher	——	——
	T. W. Campbell	——	——
4—	Marion C. Taylor	——	——
	R. L. Wintersmith	——	——
5—	John Gill	——	——
	John R. English	——	——
6—	Oscar H. Burbridge	——	——
	William Boden	——	——
7—	Noah S. Moore	——	——
	W. Cassius Goodloe	——	——
8—	J. K. McClary	——	——
	Geo. H. Dobyns	——	——
9—	R. M. Thomas	——	——
	C. J. True	——	——

LOUISIANA.

Delegates	Alternates	
Henry C. Warmouth	——	——
Thomas W. Conway	——	——
Wm. P. Kellogg	——	——
P. B. S. Pinchback	——	——
I. Hale Sypher	——	——
John R. Clay	——	——
W. R. Fish	——	——
W. G. McConnell	——	——
Cyrus Bussey	——	——
Sam. H. Houston	——	——
A. L. Lee	——	——
A. J. Sypher	——	——
Geo. C. Benham	——	——
C. W. Lowell	——	——

MAINE.

	DELEGATES.	ALTERNATES.
AT LARGE—	Wm. McArthur	—— ——
	Thos. A. D. Fessenden	—— ——
	Harris M. Plaisted	—— ——
	Eugene Hale	—— ——
DIST. 1—	Geo. F. Shepley	Neal Dow
	Mark F. Wentworth	E. H. Banks
2—	Geo. F. Beal	—— ——
	Luther Curtiss	—— ——
3—	Stephen D. Lindsey	Sullivan Lathrop
	Wales Hubbard	Edwin Flye
4—	Lewis Barker	Samuel H. Blake
	C. H. B. Woodbury	Ezra C. Brett
5—	W. P. Harriman	John D. Rust
	Ignatius Sargent	Chas. B. Paine

MARYLAND.

AT LARGE—	J. A. J. Cresswell	—— ——
	John L. Thomas, Jr.	—— ——
	Charles C. Fulton	—— ——
	E. F. Anderson	—— ——
DIST. 1—	W. D. Burchinal	—— ——
	Samuel Graham	—— ——
2—	H. Richardson	—— ——
	J. H. Longnecker	—— ——
3—	A. W. Dennison	—— ——
	Henry Stockbridge	—— ——
4—	G. W. Z. Black	—— ——
	Caleb Douty	—— ——
5—	Francis Miller	—— ——
	George W. Sands	—— ——

MASSACHUSETTS.

	DELEGATES.	ALTERNATES.	
AT LARGE	Wm. Claflin	——	——
	F. W. Bird	——	——
	Geo. B. Loring	——	——
	Henry Alexander, Jr	——	——
DIST. 1	Charles P. Stickney	——	——
	Silas Soule	——	——
2	Henry L. Pierce	——	——
	Henry B. Wheelright	——	——
3	E. W. Kingsley	——	——
	A. W. Beard	——	——
4	E. Howe	——	——
	Thomas Russell	——	——
5	R. G. Usher	——	——
	E. F. Stone	——	——
6	Wm. A. Russell	——	——
	D. W. Gooch	——	——
7	Geo. F. Richardson	——	——
	E. F. Waters	——	——
8	W. W. Rice	——	——
	Geo. W. Johnson	——	——
9	A. R. Field	——	——
	D. H. Merriam	——	——
10	R. D. Briggs	——	——
	W. M. Walker	——	——

MICHIGAN.

	DELEGATES.	ALTERNATES.
AT LARGE—	Wm. A. Howard	Giles Hubbard
	Hampton Rich	Elias Merrill
	Marsh Giddings	I. G. Wait
	Randolph Strickland	D. H. Jerome
DIST. 1—	R. R. Beecher	J. G. Hathaway
	Henry Waldron	A. P. Sullivan
2—	W. B. Williams	N. H. Bitely
	E. J. Bonnie	C. W. Clisbee
3—	S. M. Cutcheon	S. S. Lacey
	J. W. Longyear	C. Hosford
4—	Morgan Bates	S. Foote
	Geo. G. Briggs	C. W. Deane
5.—	I. H. Bingham	W. H. Hartsuff
	J. Divine	W. Jennings
6—	John H. Richardson	Jno. N. Ingersoll
	Jos. W. Edwards	Luther Weston

MINNESOTA.

	DELEGATES.	ALTERNATES.
AT LARGE—	J. B. Wakefield	——— ———
	C. C. Andrews	——— ———
	A. H. Butler	——— ———
	H. P. Van Cleve	——— ———
DIST. 1—	J. C. Rudolph	——— ———
	Jesse Ames	——— ———
2—	W. W. Scott	——— ———
	R. N. McLaren	——— ———

MISSISSIPPI.

	DELEGATES.	ALTERNATES.
AT LARGE—	D. McA. Williams	—— ——
	A. C. Fiske	—— ——
	Jefferson L. Wofford	—— ——
	Thomas L. White	—— ——
DIST. 1—	A. R. Howe	—— ——
	A. W. Pattersen	—— ——
2—	R. M. Tindale	—— ——
	J. R. Smith	—— ——
3—	Jared Richardson	—— ——
	Henry W. Warren	—— ——
4—	Thomas W. Stringer	—— ——
	A. Warner	—— ——
5—	Thaddeus P. Sears	—— ——
	Carlos Chapman	—— ——

MISSOURI.

	Delegates	Alternates
AT LARGE—	Carl Schurz	J. J. Gravelly
	Tho. C. Fletcher	Charlton H. Howe
	A. J. Harlan	J. H. Chase
	R. T. Van Horn	Thos. Bruere
DIST. 1—	Thos. J. Dailey	Wm. M. Grosvenor
	Weston Flint	John McFall
2—	F. W. Cronenboldt	John S. Cavender
	J. W. Owens	Elijah Perry
3—	Geo. C. Thilenius	Antone Hunt
	Geo. A. Moser	S. S. Price
4—	Geo. L. Childress	J. C. S. Colby
	J. H. Creighton	Geo. D. Orner
5—	S. S. Burdett	J. F. Hume
	R. C. Leaming	Joseph A. Eppstein
6—	P. R. Dolman	J. B. Waters
	J. H. Rickards	J. P. St. John
7—	David Bonham	Ira C. Busick
	J. F. Asper	J. H. Hammond
8—	A. W. Mullins	A. H. Linder
	Hiram M. Hiller	Joseph R. Winchell
9—	D. P. Dyer	G. Galloway
	John C. Orrick	Dan M. Draper

MONTANA.

DELEGATES.	ALTERNATES.
Wilber F. Sanders	James Gibson
Wm. H. Claggett	—— Willson
Geo. M. Pinney	Isaac D. Huntoon

NEBRASKA.

Silas A. Strickland	John Ritchie
Alvin Saunders	Elam Clark
P. B. Stevenson	A. J. Harding
R. W. Purnas	P. J. Majors
L. Gerard	S. C. Smith
Sam'l. Maxwell	J. G. Miller

NEVADA.

Chas. E. De Long	——	——
G. N. Collins	——	——
Lewis Hyntman	——	——
H. H. Beck	——	——
J. M. Walker	——	——
O. R. Leonard	——	——

NEW HAMPSHIRE.

	DELEGATES.	ALTERNATES.
AT LARGE—	Wm. E. Chandler	D. H. Buffum
	E. M. Topliff	B. F. Whidden
	J. H. Bailey	Henry McFarland
	C. S. Faulkner	Peter Kimball
DIST. 1—	J. E. Bickford	A. C. Currier
	Ezra Gould	Wm. N. Blair
2—	James F. Briggs	Thos. B. Wattles
	Francis B. Ayer	Geo. W. Estabrook
3—	Edward Vaughn	W. W. Russell, Jr
	Thos. P. Cheney	E. W. Farr

NEW JERSEY.

AT LARGE—	John S. Irick	—— ——
	John I. Blair	—— ——
	George T. Cobb	—— ——
	Cortlandt Parker	—— ——
DIST. 1—	W. E. Potter	—— ——
	John W. Hazleton	—— ——
2—	Robt. C. Bellville	—— ——
	Jarvis H. Bartlett	—— ——
3—	Chas. A. Skillman	—— ——
	John Davidson	—— ——
4—	Edward A. Walton	—— ——
	James Nightingale	—— ——
5—	James Gopsill	—— ——
	Cornelius Walsh	—— ——

NEW YORK.

	DELEGATES.	ALTERNATES.
AT LARGE	Daniel E. Sickles	John E. Williams
	Lyman Tremain	Gilbert Robertson, Jr
	Charles Andrews	William W. Campbell
	D. D. S. Brown	John Allen, Jr
DIST. 1	Alfred Wagstaff, Jr	Albert O. Wilcox
	L. Bradford Prince	Samuel Smith
2	Charles W. Godard	James A. Van Brunt
	Arch'd M. Bliss	William H. Burleigh
3	Joshua M. Van Cott	A. B. Hodges
	J. Reeve	Charles J. Lowrie
4	F. J. Fithian	James Winterbotton
	Joshua G. Abbe	Nathan Kingsley, Sr
5	Moses H. Grinnell	Joseph F. Ellery
	E. D. Culver	Thomas Mulligan..
6	Charles S. Spencer	Jacob L. Dodge
	John D. Lawson	George F. Merklee
7	John Cochrane	Stephen H. Knapp
	W. T. Ashman	Simon Hazleton
8	W. R. Stewart	E. Harrison Reed
	John D. Ottiwell	John Webber
9	James W. Culver	Jotham Wilson, Sr
	Charles H. Cooper	Wilson Berryman
10	H. D. Robertson	J. F. Hall
	C. M. Depew	Charles J. Gillis
11	George Clark	Halsted Sweet
	H. R. Low	John Waller, Jr
12	B. Platt Carpenter	H. G. Eastman
	Jacob W. Hoysradt	Ezra Waterbury
13	George H. Sharp	Jacob Lefever
	Rufus H. King	John B. Bronk
14	Hamilton Harris	William G. Weed
	Borden H. Mills	Weidman Dominick
15	Robert M. Hasbrouck	Joseph F. Battershall
	Alex. Barclay	Joseph Potter
16	William W. Rockwell	Robert Waddell
	Eli W. Rogers	Wm. E. Calkins
17	Calvin T. Hulburd	William C. Brown
	William Gillis	Henry A. Paddock
18	Truman G. Younglove	Charles Stanford
	Seymour Sexton	Abram Hoffman
19	E. Blakely	Matthew Griffin
	Lewis Kingsley	Frederick Juliand
20	William Dewey	James Feeter

NEW YORK—CONCLUDED.

DELEGATES.	ALTERNATES.
E. B. Livingston	Allen Campbell
21—Ellis H. Roberts	Charles M. Scholefield
George B. Anderson	Patrick C. Costello
22—Benj. E. Bowen	J. W. Merchant
Deloss W. Cameron	John H. Mann
23—Frank Hiscock	E. Hannon
R. Holland Duell	David Hibbard
24—John S. Fowler	T. G. Yoemans
A. D. Baker	Simeon Holton
25—Peter S. Bonesteel	Geo. B. Dusenbury
Isaac L. Endrees	W. H. Kelsey
26—J. W. Dwight	Alonzo B. Cornell
Thomas I. Chatfield	William Smyth
27—Stephen T. Hoyt	Charles D. Robinson
Luther Caldwell	John H. Butler
28—E. L. Pitts	John Berry
A. C. Wilder	Daniel Kingsley
29—John Fisher	James Low
Andrew W. Brazee	Thomas Corlett
30—L. K. Bass	Isaac Holloway
Fred H. James	Seth Fenner
31—George Barker	C. L. Norton
Patrick H. Jones	H. Van Aernam

NORTH CAROLINA.

DELEGATES.	ALTERNATES.
AT LARGE—Alfred Dockery	——— ———
W. R. Myers	——— ———
L. G. Estes	——— ———
DIST. 1—E. W. Jones	——— ———
2—Hiram Potter, Jr.	——— ———
3—F. F. French	——— ———
4—Jos. W. Holden	——— ———
Jas. H. Harris	——— ———
5—C. H. Carpenter	——— ———
6—J. B. Cook	——— ———
C. J. Cowles	——— ———
7—T. F. Lee	——— ———

OHIO.

	DELEGATES.	ALTERNATES.
AT LARGE	F. Hassaurek	—— ——
	John C. Lee	L. J. Critchfield
	W. B. Castle	Jacob Brinkerhoff
	James Scott	V. B. Horton
DIST. 1	W. Stoms	George Crist
	J. W. Sands	E. C. Williams
2	Thos. L. Young	F. W. Moore
	Henry Kessler	H. G. Kennett
3	O. C. Maxwell	Seth Haynes
	N. C. McFarland	Felix Marsh
4	L. H. Long	Judge Carey
	Horace Coleman	Samuel V. Taylor
5	O. T. Locke	Chas. M, Kurtz
	L. T. Hunt	I. D. Clark
6	S. Hemphill	T. F. Sniffin
	Geo. W. Hulick	W. R. Smith
7	Coates Kinney	J. D. Stine
	James S. Goode	J. M. Fuson
8	Thos. C. Jones	A. E. Lee
	H. C. Godman	W. G. Beatty
9	Fred. Wickman	J. G. Robertson
	A. B. Nettleton	J. S. Yerk
10	Asher Cook	O. Watters
	Horace Sessions	A. B. Ainger
11	John Campbell	S. P. Drake
	John Ellison	Simeon Nash
12	Geo. W. Gregg	W. S. Jones
	T. W. Beach	John L. Sheridan
13	John A. Sinnett	T. W. Collier
	Israel Green	C. D. Caldwell
14	A. S. McClure	W. C. Beer
	Jno. H. Boynton	N. H. Bostwick
15	F. W. Wood	A. W. McCormick
	Cyrus Grant	J. M. Dana
16	B. R. Cowen	J. D. Taylor
	E. Burnet	A. Simmons
17	J. C. Hostetter	Josiah Thompson
	J. F. Olivers	J. Dunbar
18	S. S. Osborne	W. Meyer
	R. P. Spalding	D. H. Brinkerhoff
19	H. B. Perkins	J. N. Hathaway
	J. N. Hathaway	Joseph Bruff

OREGON.

DELEGATES.	ALTERNATES.	
R. Mallory	——	——
H. W. Corbett	——	——
H. R. Kincaid	——	——
L. S. Thompson	——	——
J. R. Failing	——	——
Maxwell Ramsey	——	——

PENNSYLVANIA.

AT LARGE—	John W. Forney	——	——
	James U. Orne	——	——
	Thomas E. Cochrane	——	——
	A. R. McClure	——	——
	E. Read Myer	——	——
	J. W. Blanchard	——	——
	Tim. Bartholomew	——	——
	Gen'l. Wm. Tilly	——	——
DIST. 1—	Benj. L. Berry	——	——
	Jas. T. Gillingham	——	——
2—	John U. Houseman	——	——
	Daniel B. Beitler	——	——
3—	Alexr. M. Fox	——	——
	Daniel P. Ray	——	——
4—	Wm. U. Remble	——	——
	Benj. U. Brown	——	——
5—	Alfred Harmer	——	——
	Mahlon Tardley	——	——
6—	Saml. McHose	——	——
	Wm. R. Ritterhouse	——	——
7—	J. Smith Futtrey	——	——
	Saml. B. Thomas	——	——
8—	George S. Erbert	——	——
	William M. Baird	——	——
9—	J. W. Fisher	——	——
	R. L. Houston	——	——
10—	T. T. Wortt	——	——
	J. G. Frick	——	——

PENNSYLVANIA—Concluded.

Delegates.	Alternates.	
11—Saml. E. Dimmick	——	——
Wm. H. Armstrong	——	——
12—Henry M. Hoyt	——	——
Wm. H. Jessup	——	——
13—E. O. Goodrich	——	——
A. F. Russell	——	——
14—J. G. Bornherger	——	——
Franklin Bound	——	——
J. D. Cameron	——	——
A. R. Fisk	——	——
15—Kirk Haines	——	——
Hugh W. McCall	——	——
16—John Cessna	——	——
E. G. Fahnestock	——	——
17—E. Roberts	——	——
T. F. McCoy	——	——
18—Saml. Linn	——	——
Henry Williams	——	——
19—Henry Souther	——	——
Harrison Allen	——	——
20—Saml. Wilson	——	——
P. R. Gray	——	——
21—Danl. S. Porter	——	——
J. R. McAfee	——	——
22—J. R. Morehead	——	——
A. M. Brown	——	——
23—John M. Thompson	——	——
John V. Painter	——	——
S. A. Purviance	——	——
24—John C. Flenrichen	——	——
James R. Kelly	——	——

RHODE ISLAND.

	DELEGATES.	ALTERNATES.
AT LARGE—	James D. W. Perry	—— ——
	Lyman B. Frieze	—— ——
	Rowland G. Hazard	—— ——
	James W. Pendleton	—— ——
DIST. 1—	Charles C. Van Zandt	—— ——
	Lysander Flagg	—— ——
2—	William H. Reynolds	—— ——
	William Green	—— ——

SOUTH CAROLINA.

B. F. Whittemore	Robert Small
H. E. Hayne	Gilbert Pillsbury
J. H. Jencks	T. H. Rainey
J. P. McEpping	S. A. Swails
B. O. Duncan	T. T. Coghlan
Wm. E. Rose	T. K. Tilson
Carlos T. Stolbrand	W. J. McKinlay
T. W. Lewis	R. B. Elliott
M. R. Fory	J. H. Allen
E. Frask	Wm. B. Johnson..
Thomas Talbot	J. N. Newell
Cadwallader Carn	H. L. Shrewsbury
—— ——	D. T. H. Nagle

TENNESSEE.

	DELEGATES.	ALTERNATES.
AT LARGE—	Wm. B. Stokes	S. B. Brown
	T. A. Hamilton	R. Hough
	F. S. Richards	J. A. Maberry
	Thos. H. Pearne	Moses Hopkins
DIST. 1—	C. H. McKinney	A. P. Curry
	S. A. Bovell	A. S. Chadbourne
2—	L. C. Houk	N. E. Cobleigh
	R. P. Eaton	J. A. Hyden
3—	A. G. Sharp	A. S. Bradley
	W. L. Woodcock	A. J. White
4—	W. Y. Elliott	A. G. Sandford
	Wm. Bosson	Guy W. Wines
5—	T. McKinley	R. McP. Smith
	Abram Smith	H. H. Thomas
6—	S. M. Arnell	Geo. W. Simpson
	J. Jay Buck	Clay Newland
7—	Isaac R. Hawkins	J. W. Purviance
	O. F. Brown	J. J. Sears
8—	Barbour Lewis	H. E. Hudson
	J. L. Winfield	Harry S. Lee
DIST. AT LARGE—	Wm. J. Smith	——— ———
	John B. Rogers	——— ———

TEXAS.

A. J. Hamilton	——— ———
Geo. W. Paschal	——— ———
C. N. Riottet	——— ———
Oscar F. Hunsaker	——— ———
W. E. Horne	——— ———
G. T. Ruby	——— ———
Robt. K. Smith	——— ———
A. H. Longley	——— ———
S. D. Wood	——— ———
Byron Porter	——— ———

VERMONT.

	DELEGATES.	ALTERNATES.
AT LARGE—	T. W. Park	Jas. K. Hyde
	G. J. Stannard	Jed. P. Ladd
	L. Baker	Geo. N. Dale
	S. E. Pingree	H. Carpenter
DIST. 1—	W. Y. W. Ripley	Chas. Field
	G. C. Shepard	Wm. H. Nash
2—	Wm. H. Johnson	F. Tyler
	J. C. Stearns	J. Atkinson
3—	D. R. Bailey	J. A. Shedd
	W. W. Grout	——— Powers

VIRGINIA.

	DELEGATES.	ALTERNATES.
AT LARGE—	John Hauxhurst	——— ———
	Lysander Hill	——— ———
DIST. 1—	Henry A. Pierce	——— ———
	Stephen R. Harrington	——— ———
2—	John Burke	——— ———
	——— ———	——— ———
3—	——— ———	——— ———
	——— ———	——— ———
4—	Fred. M. Kimball	——— ———
	Sanford Dodge	——— ———
5—	Edgar Allan	——— ———
	——— ———	——— ———
6—	——— ———	——— ———
	——— ———	——— ———
7—	John M. Thacher	——— ———
	Thomas L. Tullock	——— ———
8—	George S. Smith	——— ———
	Minor Goodell	——— ———

WEST VIRGINIA.

	DELEGATES.	ALTERNATES.
AT LARGE—	John R. Hubbard	—— ——
	Ellery R. Hall	—— ——
	Daniel D. T. Farnsworth	—— ——
	Henry C. McWhorter	—— ——
DIST. 1—	Samuel D. Karnes	John A. Hutchinson
	Francis P. Pierpoint	R. S. Northcott
2—	Joseph T. Hoke	W. M. Welch
	Leonard B. Perry	R. W. Blue
3—	Cyrus Newlin	G. Slack
	Thomas Baggess	R. S. Brown

WISCONSIN.

	Delegates	Alternates
AT LARGE—	Edward Salomon	F. C. Winkler
	Horace Rublee	R. B. Anderson
	E. H. Galloway	Orrin Hatch
	Henry Baetz	Isaac Stephenson
DIST. 1—	O. S. Head	A. Van Wyck
	N. M. Littlejohn	S. Pratt
2—	A. J. Turner	A. Holley
	L. B. Caswell	S. J. Conklin
3—	O. B. Thomas	J. G. Clark
	Jas. Bintliff	D. L. Downs
4—	A. Scott Sloan	M. Burnham
	Geo. S. Graves	Geo. F. Wheeler
5—	E. L. Browne	A. Nash
	D. C. Ayers	G. H. Myers
6—	Chas. Seymour	T. C. Pound
	W. J. Kershaw	S. H. Alban

The question being on the adoption of the report, the motion prevailed.

MR. SANDS, of Maryland—I desire to say that, now that Maryland has been admitted to the Convention, she desires the names of those whom she has chosen as officers to go upon the roll.

THE PRESIDENT—Are they in the hands of the Secretary? If not, the chairman will please forward them. The Committee on the Order of Business is ready to report.

REPORT OF COMMITTEE ON RULES AND ORDER OF BUSINESS.

MR. BARKER, of New York, Chairman of the Committee on Order of Business—Mr. President, the Committee on Order of Business is ready to report, and I would request that the Secretary read the report.

MR. ROOT, of Arkansas, Secretary of the Committee, read the report, as follows:

The Committee on Order of Business respectfully submits the following:

RULE 1. Upon all subjects before the Convention, the States shall be called in alphabetical order.

RULE 2. Four votes shall be cast by the delegates at large of each State, and each Congressional District shall be entitled to two votes. The votes of each delegation shall be reported by its chairman.

RULE 3. The report of the Committee on Credentials shall be disposed of before the report of the Committee on Platform and Resolutions is acted upon, and the report of the Committee on Platform and Resolutions shall be disposed of before the Convention proceed to the nomination of candidates for President and Vice President.

RULE 4. In making the nominations for President and Vice President, in no case shall the calling of the roll be dispensed with. When it shall appear that any candidate has received the majority of the votes cast, the President of the Convention shall announce the question to be, "Shall the nomination of the candidate be made unanimous?" But if no candidate shall have received a majority of the votes, the Chair shall direct the vote to be again taken, which shall be repeated until some candidate shall have received a majority of the votes cast.

RULE 5. When a majority of the delegations from any two States shall demand that a vote be recorded, the same shall be taken by States, the Secretary calling the roll of States in the order heretofore stated.

RULE 6. In the record of the vote by States, the vote of each State shall be announced by the chairman, and, in case the votes of any State shall be divided, the chairman shall announce the number of votes cast for any candidate, or for or against any proposition.

RULE 7. When the previous question shall be demanded by a majority of the delegation of any State, and the demand seconded by two or more States, and the call sustained by the majority of the Convention, the question shall then be proceeded with and disposed of according to the rules of the House of Representatives in similar cases.

RULE 8. No member shall speak more than once upon the same question, nor longer than five minutes, without the unanimous consent of the Convention, except that delegates presenting the name of a candidate shall be allowed ten minutes to present the name of such candidate.

RULE 9. The rules of the House of Representatives shall continue to be the rules of this Convention so far as they are applicable and not inconsistent with the foregoing rules.

RULE 10. A National Union Executive Committee shall be appointed, to consist of one member from each State, Territory and District represented in this Convention. The roll shall be called, and the delegation from each State, Territory and District shall name, through their chairman, a person to act as a member of such committee.

Respectfully submitted,

GEO. BARKER, Chairman.

L. H. ROOT, Secretary.

MR. VAN ZANDT, of Rhode Island—Mr. President, I understand, from a member of the Committee on Resolutions, that it will be impossible for them to report before to-morrow afternoon, probably, and that will necessarily defer the nomination for President, and I am led to the opinion, from what I have seen here this afternoon, that the Convention is somewhat impatient to proceed to that nomination. I therefore hope, sir, that the Rules may be so far modified as to strike out that portion of them providing for the report of the Committee on Platform and Resolutions before the nomination of candidates for President and Vice President. And, if the Chair will have the kindness to allow the Secretary to refer to it, I will propose, with the consent of the Convention, that amendment.

THE PRESIDENT—The Secretary will read the Rule.

The Secretary read Rule 3, as follows:

"The report of the Committee on Credentials shall be disposed of before the report of the Committee on Platform and Resolutions is acted upon, and the report of the Committee on Platform and Resolutions shall be disposed of before the Convention proceed to the nomination of candidates for President and Vice President."

MR. VAN ZANDT, of Rhode Island—I move you, Mr. President, that the section be stricken out. [Cries of "No, no."] If the Convention desire to amend my motion, of course that motion is in order. I will confine it, however, sir, to the Presidency.

MR. THOMPSON, of Indiana (Chairman of the Committee on Resolutions)—I fear, sir, that the Convention may be led to act under a misapprehension. I think I am authorized to say, sir, as Chairman of the Committee on Resolutions, that you may reasonably expect a report from us very early to-morrow morning. There is no reason why we should be engaged up till to-morrow afternoon. It is right, therefore, and proper, that you should understand how we stand before we vote on that proposition.

MR. BARTHOLOMEW, of Pennsylvania—Mr. President, I move to amend the motion of the gentleman from Rhode Island, by moving that this Convention do now proceed to the nomination of candidates for the offices of President and Vice President of the United States. [Cries of "No, no."]

MR. COLES, of North Carolina—I move to lay the motion and the amendment on the table.

THE PRESIDENT—The motion of the gentleman from Pennsylvania [Mr. Bartholomew] is out of order. The motion to lay on the table is in order.

MR. COCHRANE, of New York—I ask for information whether, if the motion to lay on the table prevail, it does not carry on the table with it that portion of the report to which the amendment of the gentleman refers.

THE PRESIDENT—The Chair understands that it lays the whole subject on the table.

MR. VAN ZANDT, of Rhode Island—If I understand, sir, that the committee will report early in the morning, I will withdraw my motion. But I understand from two gentlemen near me, members of that Committee, that it will be practically impossible to for them to do so, and I, therefore, shall insist upon it.

MOTION TO ADJOURN.

MR. ———, of ——— I move that the Convention now adjourn till 10 o'clock to-morrow morning.

MR. COCHRANE, of New York—I rise to a point of order.

The motion to adjourn did not prevail.

MR. COCHRANE, of New York—[not having resumed his seat]—I rise to a point of order. Well, it's lost, that's enough.

The question was put on the adoption of the amendment offered by the gentlemen from Rhode Island (Mr. Van Zandt.) The motion did not prevail.

THE PRESIDENT—Gentlemen, the rules are before you in their entirety.

MR. VAN ZANDT, of Rhode Island—Another amendment; I desire, Mr. President, to move to strike out the words the "National Union" party, and substitute in their stead "National Republican" party. [Cries of "Good."] We fought, sir, under that flag for many years. Our brothers, and our sons and our fathers have died under it; we have achieved victory under it; we elected Abraham Lincoln under it, and we buried him under it; and I hope, sir, that we will not call this a National Union party. It means nothing at all. The Union is restored. The Union is entire, and our party is, to-day, the National Republican party, and I trust the Convention will allow me [applause], although I represent one of the smallest States in the Union, and one of a very limited number of electoral votes, to propose this, to me, very important and desirable amendment—one, sir, in which I believe all the New England States, by the side of the great ocean, will concur, heart and soul, and one in which I sincerely hope the great and almost boundless West and South will join. I move you that those rules be amended by striking out the word "Union" from the "National Union party," and substituting therefor the word "Republican," and I hope it will be done by acclamation, and that no one will dissent.

THE PRESIDENT—In the call for this Convention, it is called the "National Union Republican Convention."

MR. LOGAN, of Illinois—Mr. President, I move to amend the motion of the gentleman from Rhode Island (Mr. Van Zandt) so that, instead of striking out the word "Union," the word "Republican" be inserted before the word party, so as to stand the "National Union Republican" party.

MR. VAN ZANDT, of Rhode Island—I accept the amendment, Mr. President. I would accept any amendment that the gentleman offers, even if he wanted to change my name. [Applause and Laughter.] I want the word "Republican" in, here.

THE CHAIRMAN—It is resolved to so amend. Is that your pleasure?

The motion prevailed.

THE PRESIDENT—The question recurs on the adoption of the report of the Committee on Rules and Order of Business.

The motion prevailed.

ADJOURNMENT.

MR. COCHRANE, of New York—Mr. President, I move that when this Convention do adjourn it adjourns to meet at this place at ten o'clock to-morrow morning.

[Cries of "Nine, nine, nine."]

MR. COCHRANE, of New York—At nine, then.

[Cries of "Ten, ten."]

MR. COCHRANE, of New York—I am of the opinion that ten is better, and I adhere to the original hour.

THE PRESIDENT—It is moved that when this Convention adjourns it meet at ten o'clock to-morrow forenoon. Have you any suggestions, or any other time to mention?

A DELEGATE—Nine o'clock.

SEVERAL DELEGATES—"No! no! ten o'clock." "Question! question!"

THE CHAIRMAN—Does the gentleman move to amend by making it nine?

THE DELEGATE—No, I withdraw it.

THE CHAIRMAN—All who are in favor of the motion signify their consent by saying "aye."

The motion prevailed.

MR. COCHRANE, of New York—I move, sir, that we now adjourn.

VOICES—"No! no!"

THE PRESIDENT—Gentlemen, I am requested to announce that the publishers here have prepared and furnished a campaign song, the copies of which are here, and the delegates may avail themselves of securing a copy.

A DELEGATE—I move you, sir, that the Convention do now adjourn.

A DELEGATE—I second the motion.

THE PRESIDENT—It is moved and seconded that the Convention do now adjourn.

SEVERAL DELEGATES—"No! no! Order! order!"

A DELEGATE—I move that some gentleman be invited to sing a song.

THE PRESIDENT—The motion to adjourn until ten o'clock to-morrow is pending.

SEVERAL DELEGATES—"A song, a song."

MR. COCHRANE, of New York—I will withdraw my motion in consideration of a song. [Laughter.]

THE PRESIDENT—General Cochrane—

SEVERAL DELEGATES—A song! A song! General Logan! Speech, speech! General Logan!

THE PRESIDENT—Gentlemen, those who propose to sing, desire me to say that they prefer not to sing until after the nomination of General Grant. The significance of the request will be seen when you come to look at the song.

SEVERAL DELEGATES—Logan! Logan! Palmer! Palmer!

THE PRESIDENT—There is no motion before the Convention.

A DELEGATE—I move that General Logan be invited to address the Convention.

A DELEGATE—I move that the Convention adjourn—and insist upon it.

THE PRESIDENT—Gentlemen, the mover insists upon the motion to adjourn being put. All in favor of it will signify their assent by saying "aye."

The motion prevailed.

THE PRESIDENT—The Convention stands adjourned until to-morrow at ten o'clock.

SECOND. DAY.

THURSDAY, May 21, 1868.

The Convention re-assembled, pursuant to adjournment, at 10 A. M.

THE PRESIDENT—The Convention will come to order. Gentlemen are requested to take seats. The Rev. Dr. John P. Gulliver, of Chicago, will invoke the Divine blessing.

PRAYER.

JOHN P. GULLIVER, D. D., then offered the following prayer:

Let us pray!

Almighty and Eternal God, humbly and reverently we bow in Thy presence. At the opening of this day of deliberation and action we invoke Thine aid. Coming up as the representatives of this great people from the North and from the South, from the East and from the West, we would, like the great company about Thy throne, ascribe honor, and glory, and blessing, and power to our God.

Be thou in the midst of this great assembly. Give Thou wisdom to the deliberations that are now to be instituted. Direct all the measures that are now to be adopted.

Grant Thy special blessing upon that portion of our country which is here represented—this great political organization which, through Thy grace, and under Thy direction, has been able to accomplish so much for the land, so much for humanity, and so much, we trust, for Thee. May we remember, O God, where our great strength lieth. May we remember that as we have triumphed in the past by a regard for the claims of humanity and the great law of right, so we must triumph in the future by caring for the interests of man and regarding the glory of God.

And here, this morning, assembled in high council, we desire again to consecrate ourselves, and all the influence which is under our control, to the service of our God, to the good of our fellow-men and to the promotion of Thy law.

We recognize Thee, O God, as the King Eternal, immortal, invisible, the only wise God, high above all kings and potentates, high above all princes and presidents. Thy throne and Thy authority is over all.

We pray for our great country. We pray for those who were once our enemies. O Lord! bless them. O Lord! give them a right mind. O Lord! bring them back in loving concord into the great nationality of brotherly affection and of united action. Remember the downcast and oppressed. Grant them complete and perfect deliverance. Remember those who have triumphed in the recent struggle, and grant that moderation, and charity, and kindness, may characterize all our councils and our measures.

Now may Thy blessing descend upon us. May Thy wisdom abide in our hearts, and may the courage and strength, which God alone can give, be abundantly imparted to us, and, as at the opening of these deliberations, so now, in the maturity of their progress, enable us to say in the divine words of prayer, which our Savior taught us:

Our Father which art in heaven, hallowed be Thy name. Thy kingdom come. Thy will be done in earth, as it is in heaven. Give us this day our daily bread. And forgive us our trespasses as we forgive those who trespass against us. And lead us not into temptation, but deliver us from evil: For Thine is the kingdom, and the power, and the glory, forever. Amen.

THE UNION LEAGUE RESOLUTIONS.

THE PRESIDENT—Gentlemen of the Convention, I was informed by the Chairman on Resolutions, half an hour ago, that they probably would not be able to report before eleven o'clock. By the rules, I do not recall any formal business which can now be transacted before they report. I await the pleasure of the Convention.

MR. SPENCER, of New York—I move, sir, that the resolutions of the National Council of the Union League of America, which were yesterday presented to the Convention, and by the temporary Chairman referred to the Committee on Resolutions, take the same direction as the resolutions and proceedings of the Soldiers' and Sailors' Convention, and be spread upon our record and made part of our proceedings.

9

I think, sir, that this courtesy we owe to the National Council of the Union League of America, to which is due the first Republican ascendancy in the South, and upon whose efficiency depends, in a great measure, the success of the Republican party in the South at the coming election. [Applause.] If any of the Northern States in November next, which were carried by us in 1864, shall fail to come up to the requirements of the times, we will supply their places by Radical South Carolina. [Applause.]

THE PRESIDENT—Gentlemen, it is moved and seconded that the resolutions of the Union League, which were yesterday received by the Convention, and referred to the Committee on Resolutions, be taken up and entered upon the record of the Convention and made part of the proceedings.

MR. CONWAY, of Louisiana—Mr. President, I move that the resolutions be now read to the Convention.

MR. ——— of Michigan—Mr. President, I rise to make an inquiry. How can those resolutions be acted upon by this Convention, until reported back by the Committee?

THE PRESIDENT—The motion was, that they be recalled from the Committee on Resolutions.

MR. ——— of Michigan—I move you, Mr. President, that the Committee be requested to report those resolutions at once back to the Convention.

MR. SPENCER, of New York—Mr. President, there may be a misapprehension in regard to entering those resolutions upon our record. We shall, by entering them upon our record, by no means adopt them, but extend an act of courtesy to that body by reciting in our proceedings the fact that they sent us such resolutions.

THE PRESIDENT—Does the gentleman make his motion, then, that those resolutions be recalled from the Committee and entered upon the journal?

MR. SPENCER, of New York—Yes, sir, as a part of the proceedings of this Convention; it is a matter of fact which has transpired, which ought not to be ignored.

THE PRESIDENT—The motion now stands that those resolutions be recalled from the Committee on Resolutions, entered upon the journal, and made a part of these proceedings.

MR. CONWAY, of Louisiana—I call for the reading of the resolutions.

THE PRESIDENT—The Secretary will read the resolutions.

The Secretary then read the following communication and resolutions, from a printed copy:

CHICAGO, May 20, 1868.

To the President of the Union National Convention:

DEAR SIR: By direction of the National Council of the Union League of America, I have the honor to enclose a copy of resolutions passed by that body, in session in this city, and respectfully ask, in accordance with the request of said National Council, that they be presented to your Convention.

I am, very respectfully, yours,

CHARLES C. LATHROP, of New Jersey,
Chairman of Committee.

RESOLUTIONS

Adopted by the National Council of America, in session at Chicago, May 19, 1868:

Resolved, 1. That we deem the Union League of America of vital importance to the success of the Republican party, and the maintenance of loyalty, liberty, and equal rights in the Union, and urge its being vigorously sustained and reorganized in all the States as the right arm of the Union party.

2. That we pledge the loyal people of the North to uphold, protect, and defend the loyal people of the South from injustice, oppression, and assassination, and to this end will use all the means in our power, even the resort to arms, if requisite, in defence of their right to life, liberty, and the pursuit of happiness.

3. That we would express our high appreciation of the sublime patience, forbearance, and magnanimity of the negroes of the South, and their devotion as soldiers throughout the Union, during the war of the rebellion, and of their hearty loyalty, zeal, and becoming deportment since, showing that, under all circumstances in which they have been placed, they have justified the reposing in their hands the highest boon of an American citizen, the ballot, and illustrated the truth that it is eminently wise and always safe to act with equity and justice to all men, without regard to race or color.

4. That impartial suffrage is a cardinal principle of the Republican party, and should not be abandoned; and that we urge upon the several States, and upon Congress, the adoption of such measures as will secure the right of suffrage to every American citizen impartially.

5. That we fully indorse the action of Congress, and consider that the hour is passed for hesitation, compromise, and leniency toward those who support and defend traitors and endeavor to restore them to power, and that the loyal people of the country are unanimous in the sentiment that all who defy and trample under foot the acts of Congress for the maintenance of the principles our gallant soldiers and sailors fought and died to secure, ought to be hurled from power by the use of every loyal and constitutional means devised, and that any, whoever he may be, that has been recreant to his duty in securing this, failed to meet the expectations of the loyal people of the country, will be marked by men, and will receive the indignation and censure he so richly merits, and will be denounced in thunder tones, as an unworthy servant, whose place should be filled by a true patriot; and we especially feel called upon to condemn the traitorous conduct of the Senators who disappointed the hopes of every loyal heart in the land, in voting for the acquittal of Andrew Johnson, whom they knew to be guilty of the crime charged, and deserted their country in the hour of its peril; and we class them with those traitors to their party and country, Cowan, Dixon, Doolittle, and Andrew Johnson, with the assurance that a traitor's doom awaits them.

6. That we respectfully recommend to the Union National Convention the nomination of that tried soldier, judicious man, and reliable loyalist, U. S. Grant, for President, and of an undoubted Republican, and of a-proved experienced statesman for Vice President. With such men we feel confident of victory, as our cause is eminently that of truth, justice, and equal rights, and must be approved of God.

INFORMALITY OBJECTED TO.

MR. JONES, of Ohio—Mr. President, is not this a most extraordinary proceeding? We have a rule that every proposition that is submitted to this Convention shall be referred to the Committee on Resolutions, without discussion. But here is a motion that a resolution, or a series of resolutions that have been referred to that Committee, shall be sent for and brought back into this Convention before we have allowed the ordinary courtesy to that Committee, of waiting to see what may be their judgment upon the merits of the resolutions. Why, sir, if this principle is to be sanctioned by this Convention, then every other friend of every other resolution that has been referred to the Committee, can make a motion, either that they be spread upon the records, or some other motion, and upon the strength of that motion, a discussion of the merits of the whole of those resolutions can be gone into in this Convention, and thereby the rule of this Convention necessary for the dispatch of business (that these resolutions shall be referred without debate), will be rendered useless.

Why, sir, we do not know but that this Committee will report the very thing proposed. We do not know but they will report that these resolutions shall be spread upon the journal. We should wait and see; and, in view of this fact, and in view of the debate we shall open upon that, and the interminable discussion that will come up, upon this question, I move that this whole matter be laid on the table.

MR. COCHRANE, of New York—I rise, Mr. President, for information. What is the state of the resolutions now before the Convention? What is the motion?

THE PRESIDENT—These resolutions were regularly referred to the Committee on Resolutions, and a motion is now made that they be recalled from that Committee and entered upon the records of the Convention, and made a part of its proceedings. It is moved that motion be laid on the table.

MR. COCHRANE, of New York—I ask for a division of the question; first, upon recalling it from the Committee, and then upon its being spread upon the record.

MR. JONES, of Ohio—It is not in order. There is a motion to lay on the table.

THE PRESIDENT—The motion to lay on the table is in order.

The motion to table, prevailed.

MR. SPENCER, of New York—I move that the resolution just laid on the table be now taken from the table. [Cries of "No, no."]

MR. JONES, of Ohio—The gentleman is out of order. They are not laid upon the table at all. The whole subject is laid upon the table.

MR. SPENCER, of New York—I am in order, and I propose to give some reasons why they should be taken from the table. I move the whole subject be taken from the table. [Cheers.]

MR. SPALDING, of Ohio—The resolutions are not laid upon the table. They are not here; they are in possession of the Committee.

MR. JONES, of Ohio—The original resolutions are not here; they are not in the house.

MR. SPENCER, of New York—If I am in order, I propose to give my reasons why they should be sent for and acted upon.

MR. JONES, of Ohio—They are not laid upon the table at all. The whole subject has been laid on the table.

THE PRESIDENT—Does the gentleman move to reconsider the vote just taken?

MR. SPENCER, of New York—I cannot, because I voted in the negative; but when a subject is on the table, I suppose it is within the power of the Convention, at any time, to take it from the table, so that we may debate it afresh. I suppose the object of laying the matter on the table is to give time for deliberation, and that at some other period it may be taken up again; and if it can be taken from the table at any time, it can be taken now.

MR. SPALDING, of Ohio—Mr. Chairman, I think we have adopted the rules of Congress; if so, it cannot be taken up now.

THE PRESIDENT—I suppose it cannot be taken up until some business has intervened. [Applause.]

MR. SPENCER, of New York—I will wait, then, until some does. [Applause.]

MR. JONES, of Ohio—I move that we have a speech from our Americo-German friend, Mr. Hassaurek, from Ohio. [Applause and laughter.]

THE PRESIDENT—Will the Convention hear Mr. Hassaurek, from Ohio? [Applause, and voices—"Hassaurek! Hassaurek!"]

Mr. Hassaurek arose, in response to the invitation, and advanced to the platform.

ADDRESS BY MR. HASSAUREK.

MR. HASSAUREK, of Ohio—Mr. President, often when I traveled over the Equadorian Andes, ascending and descending mountains, in order to pass the western branch of the mighty Cordilleras, it happened that hills which I was just ascending would obstruct my vision. As I slowly toiled up their steep acclivities, I saw nothing beyond or above them. They completely shut out the horizon from my view. For the time being, they seemed to me the last boundaries of the world, with nothing to come after. But when I had passed them; when I had risen to higher and more commanding elevations; when I had reached the summit of one of those huge mountains, which towered around us in their imposing majesty, like the waves of the ocean suddenly become stationary; and when I looked down on the country from which I had emerged, where were the hills which, but a few hours before, had seemed to me the *ultima thule*—the final barrier to all adventurous exploration? They had vanished into nothingness in the valleys below. Their long chains and ranges looked like garden fences scarcely rising above the plains. The valleys between them looked like fields between their enclosures, and no barrier, except the distant horizon, shut out the wonderful prospect from my enraptured view.

Gentlemen, we are in the midst of a period of transition. Every period of transition has its difficulties, its troubles and its dangers. These difficulties may seem insurmountable to the unphilosophical, who can see nothing but the present. The weak-minded and the despondent may see nothing beyond them. But when we shall have emerged from the lower mountain ranges, when we shall have reached the lofty summit to which we are slowly, but steadily, ascending, the hillocks below will disappear, and we shall smile at our faint-heartedness, which magnified difficulties and stood aghast before obstacles which a little patience and perseverance easily cleared away.

I do not shut my eyes to the magnitude of the problem this generation is called upon to solve. The task which is to to be performed is not reconstruction, as some say. It is regeneration. How shall it be accomplished? Let us understand the subject in question with which we have to deal. There was a South, with slavery as the corner-stone of her social and political institutions, with labor looked upon as disreputable and unbecoming a gentleman; her real estate in the hands of a few wealthy families, wielding irresistible political influence; her agriculture retrograding, her cities and towns decaying, her industry paralyzed, her commerce languishing, her middle and lower classes demoralized by the baleful influence of slavery; men bred up in the belief that they were born to command, and that traffic in their fellow creatures was a divine institution; men who had been taught from their earliest childhood that a State had a right to withdraw from the federal compact, and that secession was not treason or crime, but the exercise of a constitutional privilege. [Confusion and noise in the lobby.]

Mr. President, I do not believe that this Convention is in humor, now, to hear a discourse on the political questions of the day. I was not prepared to make a speech, and I do not wish to interfere with the business of the Convention, and would rather be excused until that is over. [Cries—"Go on." "Go on."]

A DELEGATE—I beg leave to call the attention of the President to the noise in the lobby. It is impossible for us to hear the speaker, and that is the cause of the dissatisfaction. [Voices—"Go on."]

A DELEGATE—Mr. President—

THE PRESIDENT—The Chair calls upon the police and members of the Committee of Arrangements, who are about there, to take measures to correct the evil.

MR. ———, of Alabama—I hope the Chair will preserve order, that those here who know the eloquent orator may have an opportunity of hearing him, as they desire to do. [Applause. Cries of "Good."]

MR. HASSAUREK—These men now firmly believe that they have been outraged and oppressed by the Government. Vast armies have marched and countermarched over the South. The torch of war has carried desolation into her very heart. The shackles of the slave have been stricken from his limbs, and freedom has been proclaimed as the birthright of every individual breathing the air of our Republic. Here, you have two classes. The one educated in the prejudices of privileged aristocracy, still smarting under the bitterness of defeat and disfranchisement, deprived of what they looked upon as their property, reduced to poverty and extremity, and ready to fly to arms again at the first favorable opportunity; unrepentant, because not convinced, and characterized by all the wild recklessness and ferocity which the demoralizing relation between master and slave must inevitably produce. The other class, brought up in ignorance and humiliation, tyrannized and oppressed, and enjoying no rights which white men were bound to respect, just emerging from a degrading servitude, with crude and undigested notions of freedom, and, perhaps, an easy prey to demagogues, but full of gratitude to the Government which broke their chains; overflowing with enthusiastic loyalty to the flag which brought them freedom, and determined to defend their new treasure with the arms, the use of which they have learned in many a bloody field of battle. [Applause.]

I admit this is a great problem: To evoke order out of chaos; to reconcile the hostile elements in the South, while a party in the North are trying its utmost to fan the flames of discord, resentment and vindictiveness; to restore peace; to allay prejudices; to establish security amid scenes of bloodshed and violence; to direct misspent energies into the channels of industry and trade; to revive business and labor amid inveterate aristocratic prejudices; to re-build an edifice with such a predominating quantity of questionable material; and to create prosperity where ruin and decay now reign supreme, is, perhaps, the most difficult problem ever submitted to the wisdom of mortal men.

I have heard it said that the southern portion of our country are in want of a new Moses, to lead a people unfitted for self-government to and fro in the wilderness, until the old generation, with its prejudices and vices, has died away, and a new generation has sprung up under a different system of society. But, fortunately, it does not take forty years, in this wonderful country of ours, to bring up a new generation. A writer in "Blackwood's Monthly" (a British Tory magazine) once said that the Americans have a remarkable, but successful, way of blundering through their difficulties. There may be some truth in the assertion. Blunders may have been committed in our many attempts to solve a problem, so new, so unprecedented, so difficult. But even our blunders have had their lessons, and, hence, will contribute to help us through our difficulties. Let us trust to the spirit of our institutions; let us trust to the principles which underlie them; let us trust to the genius of our people; let us trust to the glorious successes of our past, for they are guarantees of a bright and happy future.

Our first task will be to understand the problem, which I hope we do. The next will be to find the proper means of disposing of the question. It strikes me that the surest and safest way will be, never to lose sight of first principles. There are certain fundamental truths upon which all science of government rests. There are certain elementary principles upon which our American system is based. Let these truths and principles show us the way. Let them be our cloud by day, and our pillar of fire by night, and we shall soon be out of the wilderness and behold the land of promise. [Applause.]

And, first, there must be peace and security. Governments are instituted for the protection of life, property and liberty. Their cardinal purpose is security. It is self-evident that a sudden transition from slavery to freedom, and such a great revolution as the substitution of an entirely different system of society, will be accompanied by great commotions; but the sooner our countrymen in the South understand that there must be peace and security, the better it will be for them and for the country. There must be no riots, no mobs, no burning of school houses and churches, no Ku Klux Klans. A Union man in Georgia or Mississippi, be he white or black, must enjoy the same security of person and property that is vouchsafed to any rebel who comes to live among us in the North. A Northern merchant or traveler must be free to pass through a Southern State with the same degree of safety with which a Southern man may travel through Pennsylvania or Ohio. Those exhibitions of violence and lawlessness, which have disgraced the South, must cease. The same liberty of speech that Southerners may enjoy in the North must be enjoyed in the South. This is a fair and a just demand. The establishment of peace and security is necessary for the South herself, and for the business and prosperity of the whole country. Without it, the South would never recover from the effects of the war. Without it, the development of its resources and the revival of commercial and industrial life would be an impossibility. Without it, the purposes of government could not be accomplished; and peace, without it, the South would be unfit for, and should not be intrusted with self-government. [Applause.]

There must be peace and security in the South; for, in addition to the fundamental obligations of all government, the loyal people of the United States are under a special obligation to protect those who have stood by the cause of the country in the hour of need. This obligation is sacred, and cannot be repudiated without overwhelming us with everlasting disgrace and infamy. The Union men of the South, who risked their all, by their devotion to the old flag; the negroes of the South, who rushed to our rescue, fought under our flag, saved our prisoners from starvation, and harbored, fed and piloted our refugees, with a self-sacrificing devotion which stands without a parallel in the history of mankind, must not be coolly, cruelly and heartlessly abandoned to the hatred and vindictiveness of those who seek to re-establish slavery in fact, after its abolition in name. [Applause.] Hence, while there are no local governments in the South, the former State governments have ceased to exist by their rebellion against the United States, it is the duty of the Federal Government to provide that security of person and property without which government itself would be a sham and a mockery—a mere machine of vexation and oppression. We protect our citizens in foreign lands; why not, also, protect them at home? Hence, if we say there must be peace and security in the South, the loyal and intelligent people of the country will indorse this demand.

But how shall peace and security be established and maintained? It can only be done by keeping a party in power which will do it. The power of the Federal Government must not be intrusted to the hands of those who have brought all these troubles over the country. It must not be intrusted to the hands of those who would unbind anarchy and remove all checks and restraints from the southern portions of our country, at a time when they most need the protecting care of the Federal Government. The power of the nation must not be intrusted to the hands of the Democratic party, which is, and always has been, the party of lawlessness, turbulence and violence. It must not be intrusted to a party which, having been the advocate and defender of slavery, is identified with all its excesses, and, by keeping alive the spirit of rebellion and insurrection, shares with Andrew Johnson the blame and the responsibility for the present state of affairs in the South. The sacred duty of protecting the helpless and defenceless freedmen must not be intrusted to the hands of those who are daily preaching hatred of race and arousing the mob by appeals to its lowest prejudices and fiercest passions. [Applause.] In other words, the wolf must not be made the custodian of the lamb, nor must the fox be appointed the protector of the hen-roost.

In the first place, then, I say, to establish peace and security in the South, it is necessary to keep the power of the Government out of the hands of the Democratic party.

In the second place, it is necessary to promote the reconciliation of hostile elements by removing, as much as possible, the causes of complaint and irritation; and to do this, we must again recur to first principles.

To regenerate the South, it is necessary to infuse into its administration a principle heretofore unknown to its policy. I mean the principle of "equal justice to all." Southern institutions were thoroughly aristocratic. It is necessary to place them on principles of democracy. I mean democracy in its higher and nobler sense, and not in its present party signification. Let reconstruction be based upon the fundamental idea of American republicanism as announced in the Declaration of Independence. I know there are objections urged—grave objections—to admitting a certain class of citizens to participation in the exercise of political rights. It is said that, as they have just emerged from a degrading and demoralizing state of bondage, they are unfit to be judges of what is necessary for, or conducive to, their own welfare. But let me answer these and similar objections in the language of Macauley, who expresses, much better than I could do, the weakness of the objections to this feature of reconstruction. He says:

"There is only one cure for the evils which newly-acquired freedom produces, and that cure is freedom. When a prisoner first leaves his cell, he cannot bear the light of day. He is unable to discriminate color, or to recognize faces; but the remedy is, not to remand him into his dungeon, but to accustom him to the rays of the sun. The blaze of truth and liberty may at first dazzle nations which have become half blind in the house of bondage; but let them gaze on, and they will soon be able to bear it. * * * * * * * * Many of the politicians of our time are in the habit of laying it down as a self-evident proposition, that no people ought to be free till they are fit to use their freedom. The maxim is worthy of the fool in the old story, who resolved not to go into the water till he had learned to swim. If men are to wait for liberty till they become wise and good in slavery, they may, indeed, wait forever."

Hence, let true democracy be the groundwork of reconstruction. Let there be no masters and no slaves, no privileged and no disfranchised classes; put them all on the same broad footing of equality before the law. Let all men have a fair start in the race of life. Let no man be without the means of self-protection, and of vindicating his own views, feelings or principles. Let there be no rightless class, no government without the consent of the governed. Let there be no odious or irritating distinctions on the ground of color or opinion.

The reconstruction laws of Congress have partially fulfilled these requirements. But to establish peace, security and reconciliation, all considerations of enlightened statesmanship command us to go one step further, and couple universal freedom with universal suffrage. [Applause.] The existence of a disfranchised class is a source of irritation and disaffection. It is a standing threat and peril to the community. It is an impediment to reconciliation, and should be done away with. I know that rebellion has committed crimes which neither God nor man can forgive, but true statesmanship requires us to rise above the resentments of the hour, however just and proper they may be. If you must punish, punish individuals, but do not punish a class. All class legislation is odious, and, in this case, may become treasonable and dangerous to those by whom, as those against whom, it is directed. We want prejudices of color to abate, and hostilities of race to wear away in the South, which will never be the case as long as the just emancipated field-hand votes, while his former master remains disfranchised. Such a state of affairs is big with the seeds of plots, conspiracies, insurrections and violence; we want the Southern whites to accept the situation; but those that are disfranchised never will. This is human nature, and easily accounted for. Hence, let them vote—white and black—and become reconciled to each others' political rights [applause]; let the strong arm of the Government maintain the

10

public peace and repress anarchy and violence, thus facilitating the development of material prosperity, and the work of regeneration will have begun. *The developments of material prosperity are important elements of reconstruction.* Let peace and security be re-established, and the tide of Northern capital and enterprise will flow into the South. Her agriculture will revive on a new basis. Her commerce will spread and prosper. New towns and villages will arise, while the old ones take a new start of improvement, and the ex-rebel, now impoverished and believing himself outraged, will suddenly discover that all this change has been for his benefit; that he has profited by the abolition of slavery; that his property has trebled and quadrupled in value; that new chances and opportunities of enriching himself are crowding around him; and that free labor, after all, is a blessing and not an injury. Then it will be that his political views will undergo a change. A man's real or supposed interests always have a most powerful influence over his opinions—in most cases powerful enough to outweigh abstract considerations of right and justice. You cannot make an ex-rebel loyal by disfranchising him; but wait till he commences to make money under the new *regime*, and he will soon become reconciled to it. [Applause.] Unfortunately, the South can see nothing without ocular demonstrations; unfortunately, they are a people without political or economical foresight, easily misled by appeals to their passions and prejudices. The history of the last seven years furnished a number of almost incredible instances of their blindness. And they are blind now, when they drive away the Northern merchant or mechanic, instead of welcoming him with open arms and thanking him for offering to promote their interests by attending to his own. But they will not be blind to ocular demonstrations, which are sure to follow a few years of peace and order, and of security of person and property.

O, that they could listen to the voice of reason. It says to them: Gentlemen of the South, the material resources of your section of the country are great; all it requires is the repression of your spirit of violence. Let order and security be maintained and prosperity is sure to follow.

But if you let ferocity and destructiveness go unbridled, you may, perhaps, escape the vengeance of judicial tribunals, but you are sure to be punished with beggary, ruin and starvation.

Your past experience, gentlemen of the South, ought to warn you against placing any dependence on, or listening to, the advice of the worst enemy you ever had—the Democratic party. In the legends of the middle ages, the devil secured wealth and success to those with whom he had entered into compacts, but it was at the final expense of their lives and souls. The Democratic party has done the bidding of the South. It has been a willing instrument in the hands of its Southern masters, but the instrument has ruined its master. The devil has enforced the price of his services. [Applause.]

By its misrepresentation of Northern character and sentiment, the Democratic party deluded them into secession and rebellion. By its false assurances of a coming reaction in the North, the Democratic party caused them to persist in a hopeless war. There was a time when submission to the authority of the Union would have saved slavery. Had the Confederates, after the preliminary proclamation of Abraham Lincoln, laid down their arms, they would have been welcomed back with joy, and the fatted calf would have been slaughtered for their reception. Their "peculiar institution" would have been left untouched; a reaction of mistaken generosity and reconciliation would have taken place, which, in all probability, would have led to the enactment of new guarantees for the maintenance and protection of slavery. But, while the Democratic party told the North, "You cannot subjugate eight millions of men," it kept alive in the Southern heart a steady hope of a Northern reaction against the war.

There was a time when rebellion, although defeated on the field of battle, might have recovered its entire political power. The fourteenth constitutional amendment would have marked no social or political change. It would have left the political balance of power where it was before the war. It did not ordain negro suffrage or military reconstruction. Had it been accepted by the South, delegations elected by rebel votes would have taken their seats in Congress, and men fresh from the rebel armies would have been elected to govern unreconstructed rebel States. Future history will look with amazement on the almost incredible blindness with which the South refused to avail herself of the opportunity to recover—with the exception of the name of slavery—everything else she had lost.

But she listened to the pernicious advice of the Democratic party and Andrew Johnson, and allowed the favorable opportunity to pass away. It was the greatest blunder ever committed by a political party since the days when God hardened the heart of Pharaoh, in order to effect the liberation of Israel. But the Democratic party is ready to inflict further ruin and misery on the unfortunate nation. It has plunged the South in a war of secession and rebellion; it will next plunge it into a war of races. Its unceasing labors are directed to the bringing about of such a horrible calamity. It fans, indefatigably, the flames of a most barbarous hatred of race. It strains every nerve to excite the passions and violence of the negro. It cudgels its dull brains to overwhelm him with ridicule and abuse. It recognizes no right in him which white men are bound to respect. It does not recognize the obligation of the nation to stand by those who have stood by the flag when everybody else had deserted it.

But, gentlemen of the South, you can no longer trample humanity in the dust. You cannot re-establish slavery, or its likeness. The negroes will assert their freedom. They will not be deprived of their civil rights. They will not surrender political rights they have once enjoyed. Beware, then, of men whom you have made brutal and barbarous by making it a crime to teach them to be human. You may organize Ku Klux Klans, and assassinate refractory individuals; but such a course is sure to lead to a terrible day of retribution. Why, then, rush on blindly to death and destruction? Why give up your country a second time to misery and devastation? Why not take warning from the past, and discard the ferocious promptings and destructive policy of the Democratic party? Four millions of human beings, who have once basked in liberty, and whose claim to justice is recognized and backed by the moral sentiment of the country, cannot forever be outraged with impunity.

Hence, if listening to the voice of reason, humanity, and your own pecuniary interests, you will discard the policy of the Democratic party, curb the spirit of ferocity and violence, put an end to the burning of churches and school-houses, and establish and maintain peace and security, the negroes will be, not your enemies, but your workmen, your field-hands, tradesmen, or mechanics, and a regenerated South will arise, Phœnix-like, from the ashes of the past conflagrations. But if, heedless of the lessons of the past, you follow the lead and policy of the

Democratic party, there will be no revival of prosperity; bloodshed and violence will reign supreme; the grass will grow on your streets; crumbling ruins will dot your country; and, in a lava stream of blood and fire, the horrors of San Domingo will sweep over the land. Then, when your ruin shall be made complete and irreparable, by your own blindness and perversity, remorse will increase the bitterness of your despair, and your misery will be galled by your recalling, at last, that you have nobody but yourselves to blame for the ruin you have wrought. Bear in mind, then, that the Democratic party is the cause of all your troubles in the South, as we owe to it all the tears and the bereavements which the war has inflicted on the North. The ancient Persians believed in two hostile spirits, Ahriman and Oromasdes, who pervaded the universe and waged eternal war against each other. The one was the spirit of good, the other a spirit of evil. In our political system, the Democratic party represents the evil spirit. It is the natural advocate of evil. It naturally attracts to its organization those that are swayed by prejudice or passion. It is a dangerous organization, which has cost the country hundreds of thousands of lives and millions of treasure. It is dangerous because of its recklessness and its formidable discipline. It is dangerous because it commands the unthinking and the ignorant, and can change its principles and policy without losing the gross of its followers. During the war, it represented the spirit of the middle ages struggling against the cause of humanity and modern civilization; and now, true to its character, it endeavors to cultivate a spirit of bad faith and dishonesty—bad faith to the creditor of the nation, and bad faith to those to whom the nation owes security and protection. [Cheers.]

The Republican party may have its imperfections and defects. Nothing is perfect under the sun. It may have committed indiscretions and blunders. Which party has not? It may have fallen into mistakes and errors, and may occasionally have succumbed to the temptations of power; but its principles are good, because they are the principles of right and justice. Though some Republican politicians may have sinned, the Republican people are well meaning, and represent the intellect and loyalty of the country. They may administer their own correctives without calling upon the enemy to destroy all the good the Republican party has done. Let us be reasonable and careful. Any party in power will be exposed to temptations; and men are but men. Let us remember that the Republican party had to deal with problems of unprecedented novelty and magnitude, and let us remember, above all, that, with all its empiricism in matters of finance of such difficulty as had never before demanded the attention and taxed the intellectual resources of the American people; with all the inconsistencies into which it may have allowed itself to be beguiled by the wickedness and perversity of a recreant President, the Republican party is the only organization with which we can now defeat the so-called Democratic party—the representative of violence, turbulence and anarchy, the embodiment of injustice, bad faith and passion, the evil spirit of our country.

No calamity could befall our country more disastrous to its peace, welfare and prosperity, than the success of the Democratic party next November. That calamity it is our most sacred duty to avert. Men may disagree on a multitude of questions, and yet co-operate for a purpose as to which they are agreed. You and I may differ about the tariff, banks, the currency, internal improvements, capital punishment, and other questions of state or national policy; each one of us may have his own opinions on matters not strictly connected with the great issue; but we should all understand that, before we can afford to quarrel on minor topics, the main question must be settled; that the integrity of the country must be firmly established before the disorganizer should be re-admitted to power; that the new edifice must be placed on imperishable foundations before the destroyer should be let in; that the roof must be put on the fabric of reconstruction, before the door of power should be thrown open to those who would not only pervert its completeness, but also tear down the walls which we have raised. The peace and tranquility, the business and commercial interests of the country; its future greatness and prosperity; its obligations of honor, justice and good faith; its position in the eyes of the civilized world—demand that the organization which alone can defeat the Democratic party, be put in possession of the executive branch of the Government for the next four years. The policy of the Republican party has not had a fair trial since the death of Abraham Lincoln. In possession of the legislative power it could enact laws, but a hostile executor defeated their interests and purposes, or barely complied with the letter of congressional enactments, while he endeavored to defeat the spirit. If it had not been for this determined opposition of Andrew Johnson, the time of Congress might have been more profitably occupied, and the work of reconstruction would now be complete. But, as it is, the great task still remains to be accomplished, and it ought to be left in the hands of those who have begun it, and with whom alone it will be safe. [Applause.]

Do not forget that a change of administration would not be a change of individuals, but a change of principles and system. Do not, therefore, call upon those to complete the restoration of the Union who have done their uttermost to destroy it. Let not the history of the last seven years be written in vain. Let not the memory of our dead be forgotten. Let us not desert the cause for which they have suffered and died. Let us not abandon our friends. Let us not carelessly and impiously sacrifice the fruits of such a costly war. Let us not give up the building to destruction on the verge of its successful completion. Let us place the ship of State under the guidance of him who has led the hosts of the Union to victory and glory, and he will safely pilot her into the harbor of peace, good will and justice to all men. [Applause.]

One word before I close. I am expected to say something about the national debt, and the questions arising out of propositions with regard to the manner and time of its payment; questions with which our opponents have succeeded in baffling and paralysing thousands, while endeavoring to divide and demoralize us. And again I say, as I said in the beginning of my remarks, difficulties that appear insurmountable for the time being, will disappear the moment we apply to them the test of first principles, which, I repeat, we should never lose sight of. Nations should be guided by the same rules of honesty and good will that regulate the conduct of private individuals; for a nation is but an individual in the great family of nations. The same considerations of righteousness that should prevail between man and man, should prevail between governments and governments, or between citizens and governments, or governments and foreigners. [Cheers.]

"Do unto others as you wish others to do unto you." An honest man will perform his obligations. An honest nation will do the same. An honest man will not keep his promises to the ear, and break them to the hope, but he will keep them according to the letter and the spirit in which they were made. The American people, having made such enormous sacrifices to maintain its national integrity, and to secure the liberty of all its members, will not sully the memory of our war, by compromising or tarnishing our national honor.

And, sir, this debt, burthensome as it may be, will soon cease to be onerous. We are on the high road to a prosperity and greatness unparalleled in the history of nations. Iron ways of steam communication will soon stretch their arms across the continent, uniting the Pacific and Atlantic oceans, and giving birth to a new galaxy of empire States. Our resources are boundless. Our mineral wealth is still awaiting development. Our Pacific coast is but on the eve of a future wealth more solid and durable than the fabulous riches of Golconda. China, Japan, India, and the South Sea Islands, will be made tributary to California and Oregon. The flood-gates of emigration are still open in Europe, pouring out over our land millions of willing hands and stout hearts, adding millions to our prosperity, and trebling and quadrupling our population. Consider what this country will be in thirty or forty years, with a regenerated and prosperous South, with a thriving and enterprising North, with a West of gigantic greatness and strength. It will then be child's play to pay our great debt. Until then, let us be honest and true. The title of American citizen is now a passport and an introduction in the Old World; let us not become a by-word and a reproach abroad, and a source of humiliation and mortification at home. Let not the mean and timid be listened to by the great heart of the American nation. Let not the name of republicanism and popular self-government be synonymous with fraud and dishonesty. Let us not disgrace the cause of democratic institutions by an unworthy example. Let monarchies and aristocracies have no reason to boast that they are superior to republics in good faith, honesty and morality. Let us not make ourselves helpless in case of a foreign war, by undervaluing or destroying our own credit by blind and selfish legislation. Let justice be our lode-star in this crisis of temptation and difficulties; and our children, and our children's children, will bless the memory of the men who saved the republic and the cause of human freedom, in the trying days of '64 and '68. [Applause.]

MOTION TO NOMINATE.

MR. SPALDING, of Ohio—It is doubtful when the Committee on Resolutions will be able to offer their report, and the Convention is becoming impatient. I move you, sir, that the rules be suspended, and that we proceed to nominate Gen. Grant for the Presidential chair. [Cries of "No." "No."]

THE PRESIDENT—The motion is before the house, and is to be disposed of by the usual vote.

MR. ———, of Tennessee—Mr. President, I move to lay the motion on the table.

MR. SPALDING—I will not put the Convention to that trouble; I will withdraw the motion.

MR. ———, of Kentucky—I move you, sir, in the absence of other business before this Convention, that that tried statesman and patriot, Gen. John M. Palmer, of the State of Illinois, be invited to address the Convention. [Loud applause.]

ADDRESS BY GEN. PALMER.

THE PRESIDENT—Is it your pleasure to hear from Gen. Palmer?

The motion unanimously prevailed.

THE PRESIDENT—Gen. Palmer will please advance to the platform. [Applause.]

Gen. Palmer advanced to the platform.

THE PRESIDENT—Gentlemen, an introduction is unnecessary. [Applause.]

MR. PALMER, of Illinois—Mr. President, and Gentlemen of the Republican Convention: I must confess that I have attended this Convention to witness, to observe, earnest action, without any disposition on my part to contribute to the volume of words that usually attend assemblages like this. As you will see, I have outlived, in a great measure, the estimate that young men place upon mere speech. [Laughter, applause, and cries of "Good."] Years ago, when the great questions before the country were matters of argument and deliberation, I endeavored, as best I could, to contribute my share to their peaceful solution. In 1861, it was resolved by a portion of the people of this country that the problems of the hour were to be settled in the most stern and decisive manner. In my way, to the extent of the power I possessed, I contributed to the settlement of those problems by arms. [Applause.] It seemed to me, at the close of the war, and it seems to me now, that the matters in dispute between the different sections of the country were settled upon the battle-field; and all that I have desired since that time is, that the logic of the battle-field should be recognized, and the decisions there made should be carried into effect. [Applause.] Years ago, in the beginning of the controversy, the question was, whether man in all parts of the Republic should be allowed to speak. I valued freedom of speech; not much speech, but freedom of speech. [Laughter and applause.] Whilst I demanded no large share of popular attention for myself, I did insist that they who loved speaking should be allowed to do it. It was denied, not only in the South, but in many districts in the North. At that time it was insisted, not only that men should speak as they pleased, and for themselves, but that men should speak for themselves and *work for themselves.* [Applause.] I believe that, while every man should be allowed to speak freely, and speak for himself, all men should be allowed to *act* freely, and act for themselves—that every man should be allowed to own himself. He should be allowed to own, not only himself, but to own his own wife and his own children. [Applause.]

We submitted that question to the arbitrament of the battle-field, and it has been decided by the sword; and, not only was that great fundamental essential doctrine established, but it was also settled as conclusively as any question could be settled, that men should not only be free in their own persons, but that they should be alike free and alike equal before the law, everywhere, in this great Republic [applause]; and the mission of the Republican party, to day, is not to discuss theories, but to give practical effect to the great doctrines established upon the battle-field [applause], not for the loyal men alone, not for the North, not for the South, but for men everywhere in the limits of the Republic; not for white men, not for red men, not for black men, but for all men. [Cries of "That's so," and applause.]

And we supposed that the voice of the American people, during the progress of the war and at the close of the war, seemed to indicate that hereafter there would be no difficulty—that these doctrines would be accepted, at least by the Republican party—would be accepted by every man—everywhere. Six months ago, what man supposed that there remained any further obstructions to the execution of the popular will? What man supposed that we were still to struggle on in vindication of these great principles? We had triumphed during the war—at the Presidential election of 1864. We had triumphed at the close of the war, in the great conflict of 1866, when Andrew Johnson appealed from Congress to the people; and the people of the country everywhere reiterated their determination that these great doctrines should be, hereafter, American doctrines [cheers] everywhere. The public voice was spoken in language not to be misunderstood. It was supposed then that every man who accepted the name of a Republican recognized these great essential doctrines, and that they were hereafter not to be resisted—at least by members of the Republican party.

There was but one thing, then, in the pathway of the people. In 1864, by one of those wonderful blunders that sometimes seem like a visitation of the Almighty in His wrath, we elected Andrew Johnson Vice President. [Cheers.] Thoughtless men may characterize it as a blunder, but thoughtful men may well wonder whether there was not some political sin concealed—whether what we deemed a mistake, was not the judgment of the Almighty inflicted upon the country; and, certainly, less than the war itself, no curse could be heavier than the election of Andrew Johnson. [Cheers.] In 1866 the distinct issue was presented to the American people, whether that "cuss"—as the phrase is—should be removed.

The people of Illinois—I speak of our own State—by a majority unheard of in our history, instructed its representatives upon that question. Iowa spoke out. Kansas spoke out. Other States spoke out upon this question. There was no possible room for mistaking the will of the people of the country. There was but one way by which all the departments of the Government could be brought in harmony. An attempt was made to impeach the President; but it has failed. It is not for me to speak of the reasons of that failure. It is enough for me, in speaking for the Republican party, to deplore that result. The removal of Andrew Johnson was demanded for the national safety. We may talk about it; we may discuss it as a judicial or a political question; but, as a question of common sense, it is that Andrew Johnson stood in the way of the peace of the country, and ought to have been removed. [Cheers long renewed.]

Impeachment—[cheers]—impeachment is the substitute of modern civilization for old-fashioned resistance and decapitation. That is all there is of it. [Cheers, and cries of "Good, good, sir."] In old times, among barbarous people, when the ruler stood in the way of the people, they took off his head. In America, under the influence of civilization and Christianity, when the ruler stands in the pathway of the peace and prosperity of the country, they, by impeachment, take off his political head. [Cheers and applause.] Nice, captious questions, borrowed from a police court, have no application here. It is enough that the interests of the millions of the American people demanded that this obstruction should be taken out of the way, and it ought to have been done [cheers; "good!"]; or, to use a lawyer's phrase, Johnson ought to have been indicted. He ought to have been charged upon the common counts, and convicted and removed.

Mr. President and Gentlemen of the Convention, there remains for us but this remedy—I speak of the impeachment as a failure—there is a tribunal that cannot be corrupted.

A VOICE—What of Trumbull? [Cries of "Go on! Go on!"]

MR. PALMER—I leave that man to that tribunal of which I am about to speak. ["Good! good!"] There is a tribunal that cannot be corrupted. [Cheers.]

We propose, at this Convention, not to indict men, but we propose to again submit these great questions to the American people for their decision. [Cheers. "Right, right!"] We expect to summon the old anti-slavery man who has struggled on amid the storm and the sunshine, amid persecution and success; the man who stood by the flag of freedom, when many of us were still halting by the way. We expect to summon him again, and ask him to go again to the ballot-box and deposit his vote for the right. [Cheers.] We expect to place at the head of our ticket the great Captain who has led the armies of the Republic through the war. [Cheers.] And we expect to summon those gallant soldiers who followed him down the Mississippi—who were present at the fall of Vicksburg. We expect to summon those gallant men who followed the flag as it ascended Missionary Ridge, and saw the flight of Bragg and his host. We expect to summon the men who marched from Atlanta to the sea; and, also, those men who so many years struggled between Washington and Richmond, and at last saw the rebel flag go down upon the Appomattox. [Applause.]

We expect to summon all these to rally under the flag of the great Captain, and we expect, then, a vote which shall place these questions where they will be disturbed no more in our history forever. [Cheers.]

Gentlemen of the Convention, I have said to you that I have no fondness for words, for the sake of words. I trust your Committee on Resolutions are prepared to report resolutions for your consideration, which shall have no uncertain sound. [Cheers and prolonged applause.] Let us make an issue just as clear and as distinct as the stars upon the flag. [Cheers.] Let us make it so distinct that in this political fight we can do as we did upon the battle-field—that when we saw the stars and stripes we knew who was following them—we knew there were friends there. Let us have a distinct, clear, well-defined platform. I do not want any mistake as to the issues to be decided by this contest.

And let me implore you, Gentlemen of the Convention—we mean to make Ulysses S. Grant President of the United States in 1868 [applause], as you did Abraham Lincoln in '64—and let me beg of you not to offer a continued, perpetual reward to the hands of the assassin, that his life may be taken. [Applause.] Let me beg that of you. Don't make a man Vice President whose character will offer a temptation for the assassination of Grant. [Applause and cheers.] Don't do that. [Great applause.] We want him to live out the four years, and, if the country demands his services, we desire his re-election. If the country shall then prefer some other public man, we wish that he may retire, and live to an old age in the enjoyment of the confidence and affection of his countrymen. And if the Baltimore Convention had not made a mistake in '64, Abraham Lincoln would, to-day, have been at Washington. [Applause.] Abraham Lincoln would have been at Washington, ready, on the 4th day of March, to extend the hand of welcome to

Ulysses S. Grant. [Applause.] That hand is at rest forever! Let us take warning by the past; let us place the flag in the hands of none but true, well-tried men.

Gentlemen of the Convention, I am done. [Applause.] Mr. President, I thank you and the Convention for your courtesy. [Cheers.]

WAITING FOR COMMITTEE ON RESOLUTIONS.

MR. COCHRANE, of New York—Mr. President—

THE PRESIDENT—General Cochrane, of New York, has the floor.

MR. COCHRANE, of New York—I am informed that a valiant soldier, just from the field of fight, is present with us here, to-day. The smoke of the conflict has rolled past us, and we would like to have the report of that gallant soldier, of the deeds of our army done in the Senate Chamber of the United States. May the Convention, sir, hear from Senator Thayer, of Nebraska? [Loud applause. Cries of "Thayer! Thayer!"]

THE PRESIDENT—Will Senator Thayer advance to the platform?

A VOICE—He has gone out.

[Cries of "Depew," "Cochrane," "Logan," "Tremain," and "Thayer."]

THE PRESIDENT—I am informed that Senator Thayer is not in the house.

Cries of "Logan! Logan!"

THE PRESIDENT—Gentlemen! Order!

Mr. ——— of Louisiana—Mr. President: In the storm of rebellion that has passed over this country, we had among us, in the Southern States, a gentleman whose voice, in defence of the Union, was often heard high above the storm; and his name is Gov. Hamilton, of Texas. [Loud applause, and cries for "Hamilton."]

THE PRESIDENT—I am informed that Senator Thayer is here.

[Cries for "Thayer," "Hamilton," "Logan."]

Mr. ——— of Louisiana—It is the desire of Gov. Hamilton that he should be excused from addressing the House to day. He is not well, and offers his apology on that ground.

[Cries—"Thayer! Thayer!" "Cochrane! Cochrane!"]

THE PRESIDENT—Gentlemen, let us have order for a moment; order! Is Senator Thayer coming to the platform?

[Cries—"He is coming." "Thayer," "Logan," "Sickles," "Tremain," "Depew."]

The Band played the "Star Spangled Banner."

THE PRESIDENT—I understand that Senator Thayer declines to address the Convention.

[Cries—"Logan!" "Logan!" "Logan!"]

Mr. ——— from North Carolina—I move sir, that Mr. Harris, of North Carolina, an able and eloquent speaker, and a man whose services have contributed greatly towards the success of the Republican party in that and other Southern States, be invited to address the Convention.

Cries—"Logan!" "Harris!"

Mr. Van Zandt, of Rhode Island—I move you, sir, that Gen. Logan be invited to address this Convention. I offered to change my name for him, yesterday. Let us have him!

The President—It is moved that Gen. John A. Logan be called upon to address the Convention.

The motion prevailed.

Mr. Logan, of Illinois—Mr. President, I must most respectfully decline to address this Convention at this time. I would desire to do so, if I felt able to respond to the call properly. Nothing would give me greater pleasure; but I hope the Convention will excuse me at the present time from so doing. I certainly have good reason for declining the call of the Convention.

Mr. ——— of Pennsylvania—I move you that Gen. Sickles, of New York, be invited to address the Convention. [Three Cheers.]

The President—It is moved that Gen. Sickles be invited to address the Convention.

The motion prevailed.

Mr. Cochrane, of New York—Mr. President, Mr. Sickles would very cheerfully address the Convention, were he present. I am sorry to say he is absent. [Laughter.]

[Cries—"Cochrane!" "Cochrane!"]

The President—There is no motion before the Convention.

Mr. ———, of Kentucky—I move you, sir, that in the absence of business before the Convention, Hon. Lyman Tremain be invited to address the Convention.

The President—The Convention calls for Hon. Lyman Tremain.

A Voice—He is not in the house.

The band played "Hail Columbia," and "Columbia, the Gem of the Ocean."

Mr. Logan, of Illinois—Mr. President, I will make a suggestion to the Convention, sir, if permitted. Inasmuch as I declined to address the Convention—I have reasons for it—I would suggest General John Cochrane—["Good, good." "Cochrane, Cochrane"]—be invited to address the Convention during the time that we are waiting. [Cries, "Cochrane!" Great applause.]

The President—Gen. Cochrane will take the platform. [Loud cheers.]

Mr. Cochrane, of New York—We are men of action, not of words. Your Committee has made its appearance. You will permit me to return my thanks for your complimentary invitation, and to retire. [Applause.]

The President—Gentlemen of the Convention, come to order. I recognize Mr. Thompson, Chairman of the Committee on Resolutions.

REPORT OF COMMITTEE ON RESOLUTIONS.

MR. THOMPSON, of Indiana—Mr. President, the Committee on Resolutions is ready to report, through its Chairman. [Voices, "Let us hear it." "Take the platform."] The Committee to whom the subject of preparing resolutions for this Convention was referred, have instructed me to submit to the Convention the following report:

The National Union Republican party of the United States, assembled in National Convention, in the city of Chicago, on the 20th day of May, 1868, make the following declaration of principles:

FIRST—We congratulate the country on the assured success of the reconstruction policy of Congress [applause], as evinced by the adoption, in a majority of the States lately in rebellion, of constitutions securing equal civil and political rights to all, and regard it as the duty of the Government to sustain those constitutions, and to prevent the people of such States from being remitted to a state of anarchy or military rule. [Loud applause.]

SECOND—The guarantee by Congress of equal suffrage to all loyal men at the South was demanded by every consideration of public safety, of gratitude, and of justice, and must be maintained [applause]; while the question of suffrage in all the loyal States properly belongs to the people of those States. [Loud applause.]

THIRD—We denounce all forms of repudiation as a national crime; and national honor requires the payment of the public indebtedness in the utmost good faith to all creditors at home and abroad, not only according to the letter, but the spirit of the laws under which it was contracted. [Great applause.]

FOURTH—It is due to the labor of the nation, that taxation should be equalized and reduced as rapidly as national faith will permit. [Great applause.]

FIFTH—The National Debt, contracted as it has been for the preservation of the Union for all time to come, should be extended over a fair period for redemption, and it is the duty of Congress to reduce the rate of interest thereon whenever it can honestly be done. [Loud cheers.]

SIXTH—That the best policy to diminish our burden of debt, is to so improve our credit that capitalists will seek to loan us money at lower rates of interest than we now pay, and must continue to pay so long as repudiation, partial or total, open or covert, is threatened or suspected. [Great applause.]

SEVENTH—The Government of the United States should be administered with the strictest economy; and the corruptions which have been so shamefully nursed and fostered by Andrew Johnson call loudly for radical reform. [Cheers.]

EIGHTH—We profoundly deplore the untimely and tragic death of Abraham Lincoln, and regret the accession of Andrew Johnson to the Presidency [cheers], who has acted treacherously to the people who elected him and the cause he was pledged to support; has usurped high legislative and judicial functions; has refused to execute the laws; has used his high office to induce other officers to ignore and violate the laws; has employed his executive powers to render insecure the property, peace, liberty, and life of the citizen; has abused the pardoning power; has denounced the National Legislature as unconstitutional; has persistently and corruptly resisted, by every means in his power, every proper attempt at the reconstruction of the States lately in rebellion; has perverted the public patronage into an engine of wholesale corruption; and has been justly impeached for high crimes and misdemeanors [good! good! cheers], and properly pronounced guilty thereof by the votes of thirty-five Senators. [Prolonged applause.]

NINTH—The doctrine of Great Britain and other European powers, that because a man is once a subject, he is always so, must be resisted, at every hazard, by the United States, as a relic of the feudal times, not authorized by the law of nations, and at war with our national honor and independence. Naturalized citizens are entitled to be protected in all their rights of citizenship, as though they were native born; and no citizen of the United States, native or naturalized, must be liable to arrest and imprisonment by any foreign power, for acts done or words spoken in this country; and, if so arrested and imprisoned, it is the duty of the Government to interfere in his behalf.

TENTH—Of all who were faithful in the trials of the late war, there were none entitled to more especial honor than the brave soldiers and seamen who endured the hardships of campaign and cruise, and imperiled their lives in the service of the country. The bounties and pensions provided by law for these brave defenders of the nation, are obligations never to be forgotten. [Cheers.] The widows and orphans of the gallant dead are the wards of the people—a sacred legacy bequeathed to the nation's protecting care. [Applause.]

ELEVENTH—Foreign emigration, which, in the past, has added so much to the wealth, development of resources and increase of power to this nation—the asylum of the oppressed of all nations—should be fostered and encouraged by a liberal and just policy.

TWELFTH—This Convention declares its sympathy with all the oppressed people which are struggling for their rights. [Cheers.]

ADOPTION OF THE REPORT MOVED.

THE PRESIDENT—The resolutions are before the Convention.

MR. SPENCER, of New York—I move, sir, that the report of the Committee be adopted. I believe that it evidences great care, and is pre-eminently a wise and truthful presentation of the articles of faith of the Union Republican party of the country, and as the great majority of this Convention is anxious and willing, promptly, in my judgment, to vote upon the platform, and as a discussion, in my judgment, would have no other effect than, perhaps, to place a dot over an *i*, or alter some word or sentence, leaving the platform substantially intact, I make this motion, and call for the previous question. ["Good."]

THE PRESIDENT—The previous question is moved.

MR. COCHRANE, of New York—I rise to a question of order. The previous question is not moved for by a majority of the delegation.

THE PRESIDENT—There is a rule of the Convention, that when the previous question shall be demanded by a majority of the delegation of any State, and the demand seconded by two or more States, and the call sustained by a majority of the Convention, the question shall then be proceeded with.

AMENDMENTS OFFERED.

MR. COCHRANE, of New York—I move you, sir, that in the resolution respecting impeachment, after the words, "properly convicted by thirty-five votes," to insert the words, "and improperly acquitted by nineteen." [Great applause and laughter.]

MR. SCHURZ, of Missouri—I am in favor of the platform as it stands. [Cheers.] I only want to move two additional paragraphs, which I think I shall have the unanimous consent of the Convention to offer. I move to attach to the second of the resolutions, a clause in relation to the right of suffrage for the colored race.

THE PRESIDENT—The motion made by the gentleman from New York is in order; will he reduce it to writing? [Cries of question.]

THE PREVIOUS QUESTION MOVED.

MR. MCCLURE, of Pennsylvania—I am instructed by the delegation from Pennsylvania to call the previous question.

MR. VAN ZANDT, of Rhode Island—I am, also, instructed by the delegation from Rhode Island to call the previous question.

THE PRESIDENT—The gentlemen from Pennsylvania (Mr. McClure) informs the Chair that he is instructed by the Pennsylvania delegation to move the previous question.

MR. VAN ZANDT, of Rhode Island—Rhode Island seconds.

MR. ———, of Ohio—Ohio seconds it.

THE PRESIDENT—It is properly before the Convention, under the rules. Shall the main question now be put? [Cries of "Yes, yes."]

THE PRESIDENT—Gentlemen of the Convention, as there is no call that this question shall be put by States, I shall proceed to put the main question. Shall the main question now be put? [Cries of "Yes, yes."]

MR. ———, of Pennsylvania—Before that is put, I wish to make an inquiry: At what point is it that the Chair regards the previous question to have been demanded? Before, or after the motion of the gentleman from New York—General Cochrane, I believe?

A DELEGATE—After.

THE PRESIDENT—The Chair is obliged to the gentleman for the suggestion. The motion for the previous question was made after the amendment offered by the gentleman from New York (Mr. Cochrane).

MR. ———, of Indiana—I understood the gentleman from New York to have moved the previous question.

THE PRESIDENT—He did, but it was not seconded.

THE DELEGATE—The gentleman from Ohio seconded the motion.

MR. ———, of Ohio—I understand the gentleman from New York, who first rose, to have moved the previous question. Ohio seconded that motion.

THE PRESIDENT—New York disclaimed having offered it as a State.

MR. ———, of Pennsylvania—It was not done by delegation.

THE MAIN QUESTION ORDERED.

THE PRESIDENT—It was not done by a delegation until after the gentleman from New York (Mr. Cochrane) moved the amendment to the resolution. The previous question refers to the amendment. Shall the main question now be put?

It was so ordered.

THE PRESIDENT—The question recurs on the amendment of the gentleman from New York (Mr.Cochrane). Has he reduced it to writing?

A DELEGATE from Ohio—We demand that the vote be taken by States.

THE PRESIDENT—Is that done by Ohio? [Cries of "No," "no."]

THE AMENDMENT WITHDRAWN.

MR. COCHRANE, of New York—Mr. President, upon my individual responsibility, I should suffer that amendment to remain; but my delegation unanimously have appealed to me, in their name, to withdraw it. [Applause.]

MR. SCHURZ, of Missouri—Mr. President—

THE PRESIDENT—Gen. Schurz has the floor.

A VOICE—Mr. President—

THE PREVIOUS QUESTION—AGAIN.

THE PRESIDENT—Gentlemen, it must be remembered that the previous question exhausts itself upon the amendment of the gentleman from New York [Mr. Cochrane], which he has withdrawn. We recur now to the main question, on the adoption of that report.

MR. SCHURZ, of Missouri—Mr. President—

THE PRESIDENT—Gen. Schurz has the floor.

MR. ——— of Ohio—I move the previous question.

MR. ——— of West Virginia—I also move it in favor of West Virginia.

MR. MCCLURE, of Pensylvania—Mr. President, I rise to a question of order. The previous question goes to the main question before the Convention, and the Convention can do nothing now but vote upon the platform as a whole. [Cries of "That's it," "That's right."] There can be no discussion; we must vote.

A DELEGATE from Ohio—I rise to a question of order. The previous question has not exhausted itself. It rests now on the main question.

SEVERAL DELEGATES—Right! Right!

MR. MCCLURE, of Pennsylvania—The main question is yet to be put.

THE PRESIDENT—The Chair has been advised by eminent parliamentarians, and reconsidered his decision. It seems that the previous question applied also to the main question, upon the adoption of the report of the Committee on Resolutions. That question is now before you. How shall the question be put on the adoption of the report, viva voce, or by States?

VOICES—"Call the States!"

THE RESOLUTIONS ADOPTED.

THE PRESIDENT—All who are in favor of accepting the resolutions offered by the Committee, and adopting them as the voice of the Convention, will please signify it by saying "aye;" opposed, "no."

The motion prevailed.

MOTION TO RECONSIDER, LAID ON THE TABLE.

MR. THOMPSON, of Indiana—The Chairman of the Committee offers an additional Resolution, as an amendment to the Report. I am instructed by the Committee on Resolutions to report for the consideration of the Convention, the following Resolution, on an entirely different subject.

MR. MCCLURE, of Pennsylvania—Before the gentleman reads the Resolution, I ask him to yield while I make a motion. I move you, sir, by his permission, to reconsider the vote just taken, and then I move you to lay that motion on the table.

THE PRESIDENT—You hear the motion of the gentlemen from Pennsylvania (Mr. McClure). Is the motion seconded. [Voices, "yes! yes!"] It is moved and seconded that the vote adopting the resolutions be reconsidered, and that that motion be laid upon the table.

The motion prevailed.

THE PRESIDENT—Mr. Thompson has the floor.

ADDITIONAL RESOLUTIONS.

MR. THOMPSON, of Indiana—The following is the Resolution submitted for the consideration of the Convention, from the Committee on Resolutions:

"*Resolved*—That the adjournment of this Convention shall not work a dissolution of the same, but it shall remain as organized, subject to be called together, at any time and place that the National Republican Executive Committee shall designate."

The Resolution was adopted.

THE PRESIDENT—The gentleman from Missouri (Mr. Schurz) has the floor.

MR. SCHURZ, of Missouri—Mr. President, I desire to offer an amendment to the second Resolution contained in this platform. I approve of every sentiment contained in it; but there seems to be something wanting. I will now read what I intend to offer as an amendment, but what I suppose the Convention may pass as an independent Resolution. It is:

"We highly commend the spirit of magnanimity and forgiveness with which the men who have served the rebellion, but now frankly and honestly co-operate with us in restoring the peace of the country, and reconstructing the Southern State Governments upon the basis of impartial justice and equal rights, are received back into the communion of the loyal people; and we favor the removal of the disqualifications and restrictions imposed upon the late rebels, in the same measure as the spirit of disloyalty will die out, and as may be consistent with the safety of the loyal people." [Cries of "Good! good!"]

This is the first amendment. The second—and I move that also as an independent Resolution—is this:

A DELEGATE—I do not think it is proper ——

MR. ——— of ———I rise to a question of order, sir, and make a suggestion, and that is, that, according to a Resolution adopted yesterday, all Resolutions that were offered were to be referred to the Committee on Resolutions without debate. That Committee is still in existence.

A VOICE—The Committee have reported.

THE PRESIDENT—The Chair decides the motion in order.

MR. SCHURZ, of Missouri—It seems to me that the platform of the Republican party ought to contain at least a recognition of the great charter of our rights and liberties—the Declaration of Independence. I will, therefore, move, if it be in order, that the following Resolution be inserted among those already reported by the Committee:

"We recognize the great principles laid down in the immortal Declaration of Independence as the true foundation of Democratic Government; and we hail with gladness every effort toward making these principles a living reality on every inch of American soil."

MR. MCCLURE, of Pennsylvania—Mr. President——

THE PRESIDENT—Let Gen. Schurz have a moment longer.

MR. SCHURZ, of Missouri—I am requested to read the first Resolution again.

MR. RICHARDS, of Tennessee—I would suggest, sir, that the Rules be suspended, that the Resolution may be acted upon.

THE PRESIDENT—The chair is of the opinion that the Committee on Resolutions has discharged its functions, and that the Convention is at liberty to receive the resolution; at any rate, Gen. Schurz has done nothing further, yet, than read his Resolution.

MR. MCCLURE, of Pennsylvania—Mr. President, I am instructed, by the unanimous vote of the Pennsylvania delegation, to second the motion for the adoption of these Resolutions.

THE PRESIDENT—Pennsylvania instructs its Chairman to second the motion for the adoption of these Resolutions.

MR. GOOCH, of Massachusetts—I ask, Mr. President, that these Resolutions, by unanimous consent, may be made a part of the platform, which we have just adopted.

Mr. Warner, of Alabama—Mr. President, as a soldier of the Republic, who fought four years for the suppression of the rebellion, and now, as an Alabama Republican, I desire to *third* that resolution [laughter], as expressing the sentiments of the Republicans of the unreconstructed States.

The President—Are you ready for the question? [Cries of "Question," "Question."]

The resolutions were then adopted.

MOTION TO BALLOT FOR PRESIDENT.

Mr. French, of North Carolina—I move you, sir, that we now proceed to ballot for a candidate for President. [Great applause, and cries of "Vote!"]

The President—The gentleman from North Carolina (Mr. French) moves that the Convention proceed to take a ballot for a candidate for President of the United States.

Mr. Logan, of Illinois—Mr. President, I rise to propound a question to the Chair. According to the order of our business, it is not necessary for a vote in reference to the nomination of a candidate for President. Is not the question to be announced by the Chair, under the rules, "Is the nomination for President now in order?" I ask the question.

NOMINATION IN ORDER.

The President—The rule for the order of business does not prescribe any specific time when the Convention will go into that business. It may delay it until after the nomination of Vice President, if it chooses. The Convention is at liberty to say whether or not it will now proceed to that business.

Mr. Logan, of Illinois—I ask whether the Convention is ready to proceed to nominations for candidates for President?

The President—Is the Convention ready? I await your pleasure.

Mr. Logan, of Illinois—Is it the decision of the Chair that nominations are now in order?

The President—They are.

Mr. Logan, of Illinois—[Cries of "Bully! John!"]—Then, sir, in the name of the loyal citizens, soldiers and sailors of this great Republic of the United States of America; in the name of loyalty, of liberty, of humanity, of justice; in the name of the National Union Republican party; I nominate, as candidate for the Chief Magistracy of this nation, Ulysses S. Grant.

The greatest enthusiasm prevailed, upon the nomination of General Grant. The mass of people arose, and gave three rousing cheers for the nominee. Handkerchiefs were waved, and the band played "Hail to the Chief!"

Mr. Bright, of South Carolina—I move you, sir, that the vote be taken by acclamation. [Cries of "No, no." "It can't be done."]

THE PRESIDENT—The Rules designate the manner in which the votes shall be taken. The list of States and Territories will be called by the Secretary, and, as they are called, let each delegation announce its choice for a candidate for the office of the President of the United States. It is understood, under the Rules, that the Chairmen of the delegations shall announce the votes of their respective States.

CALLING THE ROLL.

THE SECRETARY—The State of Alabama!

THE CHAIRMAN of the Alabama delegation—Mr. President, Alabama, through the chairman of her delegation, casts eighteen votes for U. S. Grant. [Cheers.]

THE SECRETARY—The State of Arkansas!

THE CHAIRMAN of the Arkansas delegation—Mr. President, Arkansas casts ten votes for U. S. Grant. [Cheers.]

THE PRESIDENT—The State of Arkansas casts ten votes for Ulysses S. Grant.

THE SECRETARY—The State of California!

THE CHAIRMAN of the California delegation—Mr. President, we came—ten of us—here, six thousand miles, to cast our vote for General Ulysses S. Grant. [Cheers.]

THE PRESIDENT—California casts ten votes for Ulysses S. Grant.

THE SECRETARY—Colorado!

THE CHAIRMAN of the Colorado delegation—Mr. President, the Rocky Mountains of Colorado say—Ulysses S. Grant, six votes. [Cheers.]

THE PRESIDENT—Colorado casts six votes for Ulysses S. Grant.

THE SECRETARY—The State of Connecticut!

THE CHAIRMAN of the Connecticut delegation—Mr. President, Connecticut unconditionally surrenders her twelve votes for Ulysses S. Grant. [Cheers.]

THE PRESIDENT—Connecticut casts twelve votes for Ulysses S. Grant.

THE SECRETARY—Dakota!

THE CHAIRMAN of the Dakota delegation—Mr. President, Ulysses S. Grant—two votes.

THE PRESIDENT—Dakota casts two votes for Ulysses S. Grant.

THE SECRETARY—The State of Delaware!

THE CHAIRMAN of the Delaware delegation—Mr. President, the State of Delaware casts six votes for Ulysses S. Grant.

THE PRESIDENT—Delaware casts six votes for Ulysses S. Grant.

THE SECRETARY—The District of Columbia!

THE CHAIRMAN of the District of Columbia delegation—The District of Columbia gives her two votes for Ulysses S. Grant.

THE PRESIDENT—The District of Columbia gives two votes for Ulysses S. Grant.

THE SECRETARY—The State of Florida!

THE CHAIRMAN of the Florida delegation—Mr. President, Florida, the land of flowers, gives six votes for Ulysses S. Grant. [Cheers.]

THE PRESIDENT—The State of Florida gives six votes for Ulysses S. Grant.

THE SECRETARY—The State of Georgia!

THE CHAIRMAN of the Georgia delegation—Mr. President, the Republicans of Georgia, many of whom were original secessionists, recognizing the wisdom of the maxim, "Enemies in war, in peace, friends," and ardently desiring a speedy restoration of union, harmony, peace, and good government, instruct me, through their representatives here, to cast eighteen votes for Gen. Ulysses S. Grant. [Cheers.]

THE PRESIDENT—The State of Georgia gives eighteen votes for Ulysses S. Grant.

THE SECRETARY—The Territory of Idaho!

THE CHAIRMAN of the Idaho delegation—Mr. President, the Territory of Idaho gives two votes for Gen. Ulysses S. Grant.

THE SECRETARY—The State of Illinois!

THE CHAIRMAN of the Illinois delegation—Mr. President, the State of Illinois gives thirty-two for Ulysses S. Grant. [Cheers.]

THE PRESIDENT—The State of Illinois gives thirty-two votes for Ulysses S. Grant. [Cheers.]

THE SECRETARY—The State of Indiana!

THE CHAIRMAN of the Indiana delegation—The State of Indiana gives twenty-six votes for Ulysses S. Grant. [Cheers.]

THE PRESIDENT—The State of Indiana gives twenty-six votes for Ulysses S. Grant.

THE SECRETARY—The State of Iowa!

THE CHAIRMAN of the Iowa delegation—Mr. President, Iowa gives sixteen votes for Ulysses S. Grant, and promises to back it up with forty thousand majority. [Cheers.]

THE PRESIDENT—The State of Iowa gives sixteen votes for Ulysses S. Grant.

THE SECRETARY—The State of Kansas!

THE CHAIRMAN of the Kansas delegation—Mr. President, Kansas—the "John Brown" State—gives six votes for Ulysses S. Grant. [Applause and laughter.]

THE PRESIDENT—The State of Kansas gives six votes for Ulysses S. Grant.

THE SECRETARY—The State of Kentucky!

THE CHAIRMAN of the Kentucky delegation—Mr. President, the State of Kentucky has directed its delegation to cast its vote—twenty-two votes—for Ulysses S. Grant. [Cheers.]

THE PRESIDENT—The State of Kentucky gives twenty-two votes for Ulysses S. Grant.

THE SECRETARY—The State of Louisiana!

THE CHAIRMAN of the Louisiana delegation—Mr. President, the State of Louisiana casts fourteen votes for General Ulysses S. Grant, and we propose to "fight it out on this line if it takes all summer." [Applause.]

THE PRESIDENT—Louisiana gives fourteen votes for Ulysses S. Grant.

THE SECRETARY—The State of Maine!

THE CHAIRMAN of the Maine delegation—Mr. President, Maine gives fourteen votes for Ulysses S. Grant. [Cheers.]

THE PRESIDENT—Maine gives fourteen votes for Ulysses S. Grant.

THE SECRETARY—The State of Maryland!

THE CHAIRMAN of the Maryland delegation—Mr. President, believing that our great Captain will crush treason in the Cabinet as he crushed it in the field, "Maryland, my Maryland," gives fourteen votes for Ulysses S. Grant. [Applause.]

THE PRESIDENT—Maryland gives fourteen votes for Ulysses S. Grant.

THE SECRETARY—The State of Massachusetts!

THE CHAIRMAN of the Massachusetts delegation—Mr. President, the State of Massachusetts casts twenty-four votes for Ulysses S. Grant.

THE PRESIDENT—Massachusetts casts twenty-four votes for Ulysses S. Grant. [Cheers.]

THE SECRETARY—The State of Michigan!

THE CHAIRMAN of the Michigan delegation—Mr. President, the State of Michigan, following the State of Massachusetts, gives sixteen votes for Ulysses S. Grant. [Cheers.]

THE PRESIDENT—Michigan gives sixteen votes for Ulysses S. Grant.

THE SECRETARY—The State of Minnesota!

THE CHAIRMAN of the Minnesota delegation—Mr. President, Minnesota, the North Star State, gives all she has—eight votes—for Ulysses S. Grant. [Applause.]

THE PRESIDENT—Minnesota gives eight votes for Ulysses S. Grant.

THE SECRETARY—The State of Mississippi!

THE CHAIRMAN of the Mississippi delegation—Mr. President, the State of Mississippi, the home of Jefferson Davis, repudiates that traitor, and offers her fourteen votes for Ulysses S. Grant. [Applause.]

THE PRESIDENT—Mississippi gives fourteen votes for Ulysses S. Grant.

THE SECRETARY—The State of Missouri!

THE CHAIRMAN of the Missouri delegation—Mr. President, the State Convention of Missouri instructed the delegation to vote for Ulysses S. Grant upon a radical platform. We have the radical platform, and, with full confidence that General Grant will carry it out, Missouri gives General Grant twenty-two votes. [Cheers.]

THE PRESIDENT—Missouri gives twenty-two votes for Ulysses S. Grant.

THE SECRETARY—The Territory of Montana!

THE CHAIRMAN of the Montana delegation—The mountains of Montana, and the Columbia river, are vocal with the name of Grant. She gives him two votes. [Applause.]

THE PRESIDENT—Montana gives two votes for Ulysses S. Grant.

THE SECRETARY—The State of Nebraska!

THE CHAIRMAN of the Nebraska delegation—Mr. President, Nebraska, the last State admitted into the Union, and the first to adopt impartial suffrage [applause], gives six votes for Ulysses S. Grant. [Cheers.]

THE PRESIDENT—Nebraska gives six votes for Ulysses S. Grant.

THE SECRETARY—The State of Nevada!

THE CHAIRMAN of the Nevada delegation—Mr. President, the Silver State has but six votes to give, but it proposes soon to be able to have six more to give. It gives all it has for Grant. [Cheers.]

THE PRESIDENT—Nevada gives six votes for Ulysses S. Grant.

THE SECRETARY—The State of New Hampshire!

THE CHAIRMAN of the New Hampshire delegation—Mr. President, New Hampshire gives ten votes for Ulysses S. Grant. [Cheers.]

THE PRESIDENT—New Hampshire gives ten votes for Ulysses S. Grant.

THE SECRETARY—The Territory of New Mexico!

New Mexico did not respond.

THE SECRETARY—The State of New Jersey!

THE CHAIRMAN of the New Jersey delegation—Mr. President, the New Jersey delegation, instructed by her Convention—and in giving those instructions, she spoke the voice of every man of the Republican party within her borders—now deliver their fourteen votes for Ulysses S. Grant, not only a victorious soldier, but a man, conspicuous for calmness of judgment, sincerity of patriotism, and personal honesty. [Cheers.]

THE SECRETARY—The State of New York!

THE CHAIRMAN of the New York delegation—The State of New York gives sixty-six votes for Ulysses S. Grant.

THE PRESIDENT—The State of New York gives sixty-six votes for Ulysses S. Grant.

THE SECRETARY—The State of North Carolina!

THE CHAIRMAN of the North Carolina delegation—Mr. President, North Carolina, known as the land of the "tar heels" [great laughter], gives eighteen votes for Ulysses S. Grant, and will give twice eighteen—thirty-six thousand votes—all of which will stick! [Great applause.]

THE PRESIDENT—North Carolina gives eighteen votes for Ulysses S. Grant.

THE SECRETARY—The State of Ohio!

THE CHAIRMAN of the Ohio delegation—Mr. President, Ohio has the honor of being the mother of our great Captain. Ohio is in line, and on that line Ohio proposes following this great Captain, that never knew defeat; to fight it out through the summer, and in the autumn, at the end of the great contest, and to be first in storming the intrenchments, until victory shall be secured, and all the stars that glitter in the firmament of our glorious constellation shall again be restored to their proper order, and all the sons of freedom throughout the whole earth shall shout for joy. ["Good! good!"] Ohio gives forty-two votes for U. S. Grant. [Cheers.]

THE PRESIDENT—Ohio casts forty-two votes for Ulysses S. Grant.

THE SECRETARY—The State of Oregon!

THE CHAIRMAN of the Oregon delegation—Mr. President, the State of Oregon—the most Northwestern State of this Union—have directed their delegates here to cast six votes for U. S. Grant. [Cheers.]

THE SECRETARY—The State of Pennsylvania!

THE CHAIRMAN of the Pennsylvania delegation—The State of Pennsylvania casts fifty-two votes for Ulysses S. Grant.

THE PRESIDENT—The State of Pennsylvania casts fifty-two votes for Ulysses S. Grant.

THE SECRETARY—The State of Rhode Island!

THE CHAIRMAN of the Rhode Island delegation—Little Rhody, small in stature, but patriotic, gives her eight votes for Gen. Ulysses S. Grant, and wishes she had more. [Applause.]

THE PRESIDENT—Rhode Island casts eight votes for Ulysses S. Grant.

THE SECRETARY—The State of South Carolina!

THE CHAIRMAN of the South Carolina delegation—The State of South Carolina, the birth place and home of John C. Calhoun, and the doctrine of State rights—first to withdraw herself from the Union—directs me, through her representatives sent here by a Republican majority of forty-three thousand four hundred and seventy [applause], returning as we do to the councils of those who desired only to preserve the Union, arm in arm and heart to heart with Massachusetts [great cheers], gives her twelve votes for Gen. Ulysses S. Grant. [Immense applause.]

THE PRESIDENT—The State of South Carolina gives twelve votes for Ulysses S. Grant.

THE SECRETARY—The State of Tennessee!

THE CHAIRMAN of the Tennessee delegation—Mr. President, Tennessee, being one of the Southern States that was forced into the rebellion—Tennessee, being the first to reconstruct or be reconstructed, and be readmitted into the Union, and to-day being in the enjoyment of a most liberal Republican government, casts her twenty votes for Ulysses S. Grant [cheers]; and with the solemn pledge, never again to present the name, for President or Vice President, of such a traitor as Andrew Johnson. [Loud cheers.]

THE PRESIDENT—Tennessee gives twenty votes for Ulysses S. Grant.

THE SECRETARY—The State of Texas!

THE CHAIRMAN of the Texas delegation—Mr. President, Texas, through her delegates here assembled, has instructed me to cast twelve votes for Ulysses S. Grant, from the empire State of the South, having a territory of two hundred and seventy-five thousand square miles, and capable of sustaining twenty millions of people. [Applause.]

THE PRESIDENT—Texas gives twelve votes for Ulysses S. Grant.

THE SECRETARY—The State of Vermont!

THE CHAIRMAN of the Vermont delegation—Mr. President, the Republicans of Vermont, through their delegation, give their ten votes for Ulysses S. Grant.

THE PRESIDENT—Vermont gives ten votes for Ulysses S. Grant.

THE SECRETARY—The State of Virginia!

THE CHAIRMAN of the Virginia delegation—Mr. President, the State of New Virginia, rising from the grave that Gen. Grant dug for her in the Appomattox, in 1865, comes up here with her twenty votes and enlists under his banner, and they propose in next November to "move on the enemy's works." [Loud applause.]

THE PRESIDENT—Virginia casts ten votes for Ulysses S. Grant.

THE SECRETARY—West Virginia!

THE CHAIRMAN of the West Virginia delegation—Mr. President, West Virginia, a corner of the rebellion which never gave a Democratic majority, gives freely and willingly her ten votes for Ulysses S. Grant for President. [Applause.]

THE PRESIDENT—West Virginia gives ten votes for Ulysses S. Grant.

THE SECRETARY—The State of Wisconsin!

THE CHAIRMAN of the Wisconsin delegation—Mr. President, Wisconsin, the last on the roll of States, adds her voice to that of her sister States, and gives her sixteen votes for Ulysses S. Grant. [Applause.]

THE PRESIDENT—Wisconsin gives sixteen votes for Ulysses S. Grant, and the roll is completed.

GENERAL GRANT DECLARED UNANIMOUSLY NOMINATED.

Gentlemen of the Convention, you have six hundred and fifty votes. You have given six hundred and fifty votes for Ulysses S. Grant. [Tremendous applause.]

The audience gave three enthusiastic cheers for General Grant.

THE BALLOT.

The ballot stood as follows:

Alabama	18
Arkansas	10
California	10
Colorado	6
Connecticut	12
Delaware	6
Dakota	2
District of Columbia	2
Florida	6
Georgia	18
Idaho	2
Illinois	32
Indiana	26
Iowa	16
Kansas	6
Kentucky	22
Louisiana	14
Maine	14
Maryland	14
Massachusetts	24
Michigan	16
Minnesota	8
Mississippi	14
Missouri	22
Montana	2
Nebraska	6
Nevada	6
New Hampshire	10
New Jersey	14
New York	66
North Carolina	18
Ohio	42
Oregon	6
Pennsylvania	52
Rhode Island	8
South Carolina	12
Tennessee	20
Texas	12
Vermont	10
Virginia	20
West Virginia	10
Wisconsin	16
Total	650

MR. ———, of Indiana—I move you that we try our throats with three times three, with swinging hats and waving handkerchiefs, for General Grant.

Nine tremendous cheers were given.

The band played "The Battle Cry of Freedom," and the whole Convention joined in the chorus:

"The Union forever, hurrah boys, hurrah;
Down with the traitor, and up with the stars;
And we'll rally round the flag, boys,
Rally once again,
Shouting the battle-cry of freedom!"

THE PRESIDENT—The Convention will come to order.

MR. SEYMOUR, of Wisconsin—I move that the President of the Convention be authorized and requested to telegraph the result of the vote just taken to General Grant. [Cheers.]

The motion unanimously prevailed.

SONG.

Chaplain Lozier, Chaplain McCabe and Major H. G. Lombard then sang a song written for the occasion by Mr. Geo. F. Root, entitled, "We'll Fight it Out Here, on the Old Union Line," which was received with applause.

We'll rally again to the standard we bore
O'er battle-fields crimson and gory,
Shouting "hail to the chief" who in freedom's fierce war,
Hath covered that banner with glory.

CHORUS—Then rally again, then rally again,
With the soldier, and sailor, and bummer,
And we'll fight it out here, on the old union line,
No odds if it takes us all summer.

We'll rally again, by the side of the men,
Who breasted the conflict's fierce rattle,
And they'll find us still true, who were true to them then
And bade them "God speed" in the battle.

We'll rally again, and "that flag of the free"
Shall stay where our heroes have placed it,
And ne'er shall they govern, on land or on sea,
Whose treason hath spurned and disgraced it.

We'll rally again, and our motto shall be,
What ever the nation that bore us,
God bless that old banner, "the flag of the free,"
And all who would die with it o'er us.

THE PRESIDENT—The chair awaits the pleasure of the Convention.

MOTION TO BALLOT FOR VICE PRESIDENT.

MR. SCHOFIELD, of New York—Mr. President, I move that, in accordance with the rules adopted by the Convention, the Convention proceed to vote for a candidate for Vice President of the United States.

MR. HAMILTON, of Virginia—I move you, sir, as a substitute for the motion just made, that this Convention do now adjourn until five o'clock. [Loud cries of "No! no! no! no!"]

THE PRESIDENT—Does the gentleman press the motion?

MR. HAMILTON, of Virginia—No! I withdraw it.

THE PRESIDENT—The order before the Convention, under the rules, is the nomination of a candidate for the Vice Presidency. Those who would proceed to the business next in order, will say "aye." Those opposed, "no."

The motion prevailed.

MR. PIERCE, of Virginia—Mr. Chairman—

THE PRESIDENT—Mr. Pierce, of Virginia. Attention!

NOMINATIONS.

MR. PIERCE, of Virginia—I am instructed, sir, by the loyal people of the State of Virginia, through their representatives, here assembled—

THE PRESIDENT—Order!

VIRGINIA NOMINATES HENRY WILSON FOR VICE PRESIDENT.

MR. PIERCE—To place in nomination the name of a noble son of New England as a candidate for the office of Vice President of the United States. That name is the name of the Hon. Henry Wilson, of Massachusetts. [Applause.] And, in placing him in nomination, we deem it due to ourselves—the duty of Virginia's sons as a slight reparation for the wrongs done by her in the past—for the contumely which has been heaped upon Massachusetts in the past, and as a proof of our regeneration, and as a proof that when the stone was rolled away from our doors—

THE PRESIDENT—Will the gentleman suspend his remarks for a moment. It is exceedingly difficult for the speaker to be heard. There must be better order. Proceed!

MR. PIERCE resumed—We wish to present this name as a proof that when the stone was rolled away from the door of the sepulchre that secession and rebellion had hurled us in, that we resurrected a loyal community, and that we acknowledge the supremacy of puritanical principle that had been rolled over Virginia. We now believe, that, if his name shall be put upon the ticket, it will be responded to by the loyal millions of the South, by the loyal soldiery of the country, by all those who have experienced and received the blessings that have resulted from his noble labors for eight years as the Chairman of the Committee on Military Affairs in the Senate.

We believe it would add a tower of strength. You have willed us Grant, and if you will now grant us Wilson [laughter], we can carry the election. [Applause.]

MR. BROWN, of Pennsylvania—I move, sir, that the delegates have leave to nominate the name of candidates for the Vice Presidency, but that discussion as to the merits of candidates shall not be in order. [Cries of "No! no!"] I modify my motion by asking that the discussion be limited to five minutes. [Cries—"The Rule! The Rule!"]

THE PRESIDENT—The Rule, as adopted, provides for that, unless the gentleman wishes to move a supension of the Rule.

MR. BROWN, of Pennsylvania—Will the President read the Rule.

THE PRESIDENT—The Rule is as follows:

"No member shall speak more than once on the same subject, nor longer than five minutes, without the unanimous consent of the Convention, except that delegates presenting the name of a candidate, shall be allowed ten minutes to present the name of a candidate.

MR. BROWN—I did not know, Mr. President, that there was such a Rule. I had forgotten it.

MASSACHUSETTS SECONDS THE NOMINATION OF HENRY WILSON.

MR. CLAFLIN, of Massachusetts—Mr. President, in accordance with the instructions of the State Convention of Massachusetts, in behalf of her delegation, I second the motion of the gentleman from the State of Virginia. Massachusetts has never appeared with a candidate in a National Convention of the Republican party; and she does not appear to day for herself, but she appears because she has a candidate whom she believes is national; and that, were he in any other State, that State would have presented him to the Convention either in the past or the present, and he would have been accepted as the unanimous voice of the Convention; for the people of Massachusetts know and appreciate Henry Wilson. Born in a neighboring State—coming to Massachusetts at an early day—surrounded by unfavorable circumstances in early life, he soon took an advanced position among the cultivated, among the old and well-established names of political aspirants of that State. Soon he advanced into the National Legislature, and for the last fifteen years he has occupied a seat. He has been in the Legislature of his State, and for the last fifteen years he has occupied a position in the Senate of the United States. And I challenge any man here to point to a vote of Henry Wilson, which has been against the Union, which has ever been questioned by the loyal people of his State, or which has been in favor of treason, or which has ever been sullied by treachery. And I challenge the name of any man of greater merit throughout our State and Union. He has spent more time, and done more labor, than almost any other man that can be found in the United States. In the ripeness of his life, in the vigor of his manhood, with integrity and courage, with a heart full of humanity for all men, with a genius almost unparalleled, we present him as our nominee before this Convention, knowing that he is in hearty accord with the great Captain you have placed at the head of your ticket—a man who will do more work in the coming campaign than almost any other man whom we can put forward. [Applause.]

INDIANA NOMINATES SCHUYLER COLFAX FOR VICE PRESIDENT.

MR. LANE, of Indiana—I am instructed by the delegates of Indiana, to present that tried and trusted, and true patriot, Schuyler Colfax. [Prolonged cheers.] Of the purity of his life, in private and in public—of his distinguished public services—his long identification with Congressional action—it is idle and unnecessary that I should go into any lengthy eulogy. He is an Indianian, near to our home, near to our hearts. We know him; we love him; the people are united for him, and speak with but one voice. There are no dissensions there, no feuds to heal. He is the choice of the people, and although his residence is in Indiana, his fame, thank God, belongs to the whole continent. [Prolonged cheers.]

To his past history I need but refer for a moment. He began public service, an orphan boy, with no inheritance except those gifts—those God-endowed gifts—which marked him from the beginning, a master and leader of men. [Cheers.] He began his career as a Whig politician, under the standard of that pure and incorruptible patriot, that far-seeing statesman, that representative of American character, that pure and fearless orator, Henry Clay. [Loud Cheers.] Faithful to his friends, faithful to his country, faithful to his party allegiance, he has supported every candidate of the Whig party, and every nomination of the Republican party.

These are some of his claims to your confidence and consideration. He has supported every measure of congressional reconstruction. With other distinguished gentlemen, presented for the same office, we have no quarrel. They are sons of a proud Republic. Their glory is a part of our common inheritance. We have no word of disparagement for them. When you make your nomination, we wish to be free to roll up our sleeves in their behalf; but I assure the Convention that, with Schuyler Colfax as our standard-bearer, we shall carry Indiana—sometimes, slanderously (by evil-minded persons) called a doubtful state [laughter]—we shall carry Indiana; we shall triumph in the election. We may do this with others. I trust, if another is nominated, we shall. But, with him, we regard it absolutely certain. It is an auspicious time to present a young man, a man representing the religious and moral sentiment of the country, and to a great extent a chosen, tried and true leader—no doubtful man. The painful experiences of the past have admonished us, and we must have no doubtful man in the office of Vice President. We present you no doubtful man. He has stood by reconstruction. Thank God, he has stood, also by impeachment [applause]; and when the seven recreant Senators—unlike the seven golden candlesticks burning in the old Jewish temple—when their lights shall have been extinguished, or when they shall be only dark lanterns, whose illumination is only seen in places fit for the light of dark lanterns, Schuyler Colfax, as Vice President, or as Speaker, or as Member of Congress, will be found true to his principles, true to the interest of the Republican party, and of the Union party—for they are synonymous—one and the same.

And, now that we have passed through the conflict of war, and have emerged from the storm-cloud of trouble, we shall redeem the whole United States, represented, and properly represented, and the Scripture is now being fulfilled, that even Ethiopia is stretching out her arms.

NEW JERSEY SECONDS THE NOMINATION OF SCHUYLER COLFAX.

MR. PARKER, of New Jersey—Mr. President, the Republican Convention of New Jersey gave to their delegates an instruction which they have fulfilled. A subsequent Resolution, upon the subject of the Vice Presidency, expressly declared that upon that subject no instruction should be given, except that it was the duty of the delegates to aim at the nomination of the man most fitting to occupy the place of Vice President, most fitting from his record in the past, and most reliable in the future, without regard to locality. [Applause.] In the spirit of that Resolution, these delegates are here to day.

We have a man among ourselves whom we should be glad to prefer. We have a man in the East for whom we feel veneration and affection, upon whom we can rely, and whom the country has relied upon, through the dark years of the fearful struggle we have passed through. But, looking through all the candidates before this Convention, looking through all the men of the nation, north, south, east, and west, we have determined, and, I, as their Chairman, am instructed to nominate to this Convention, for the Vice Presidency, Schuyler Colfax.

We nominate him as a young man, likely, in the providence of God, to be faithful to his country; and, in the call of the Master, to stand up ready to endure the work that has prostrated one, and would have prostrated, perhaps, another President, if the hand of the assassin had not found his heart. [Sensation.] We nominate him as a candidate of the young men. He is their representative, loved by them, possessing all the charms of heart, and the distinctions of mind, which would cause him to be known as a true patriot, as we have all of us known him to be. We nominate him because, coming from the great and growing West, we believe that he will add glory to the galaxy of men which the West has furnished, and will add even to the strength of the campaign for President, with whom, if our wishes are followed, he will be joined. [Applause.] We nominate him because we know that, in our own State, we can lift the misrule that has been over us, and we can be a Republican State. Under his rule, we can do it. Schuyler Colfax, comes up here of Jersey blood [Applause], blood that has flowed throughout this land, and is always good and true. We nominate him for the virtues that have been expressed by the gentleman from Indiana. [Cries of "Time! time!"]

MR.———, of Pennsylvania—Mr. President, I rise to a question of order. If I understand the reading of the Rules, and the intention of the Committee in reporting them, it was that there should be one speech of ten minutes allowed in nominating Candidates. That was my understanding at the time, and I raise that point.

THE PRESIDENT—I see nothing but what is contained in the eighth Rule, that there should be allowed ten minutes to announce, and five minutes in speaking afterward.

A DELEGATE—I understand that to be the rule.

THE PRESIDENT—That is the way the Rules read.

THE CHAIRMAN OF COMMITTEE ON RULES—The Rules say that the first speaker shall have ten minutes, and every other speaker five minutes. It has been incorrectly printed in the paper. It was especially talked of in the Committee, and was so understood.

THE PRESIDENT—By general consent, it will be agreed that that shall be the rule.

MICHIGAN SECONDS THE NOMINATION OF SCHUYLER COLFAX.

MR. CUTCHEON, of Michigan—I rise in behalf of the electors and delegates of the Republican party of Michigan, to support the nomination of Schuyler Colfax. [Cheers.] At the State Convention, where the Republican party was very fully represented, when the name of Schuyler Colfax was proposed for the candidate for the office of Vice President, there we witnessed some such scene as has been witnessed here to-day when Ulysses S. Grant was declared the unanimous choice of this Convention for President. [Cheers.] In Michigan, we have watched the course of Schuyler Colfax, who lives just upon her borders, and we believe, there, that no name can be proposed to the people of the United States for this high office that will excite so great enthusiasm in the State of Michigan. We know that in the State of Michigan the name of Schuyler Colfax is powerful. [Cheers and great applause.] While we pledge, sir, the most hearty support to any nominee of this Convention, we feel that, with Gen. Grant and Schuyler Colfax, we can promise for ourselves that in the State of Michigan we can roll up thirty thousand majority. [Applause.] We esteem him as true to principles as the needle to the pole. We trust him; we love him as the people all love the name of that man who comes so close to their hearts.

MR. McCLURE, of Pennsylvania—I desire to make a motion with reference to that Rule, that I think would be acceptable. If the delegates shall obey the respective instructions they have received, there shall be no less than ten or a dozen candidates presented for Vice President. I move that the Rule of order be made to read that any persons presenting the name of any candidate for Vice President shall speak ten minutes in support of the same, and that there shall be only one speech of five minutes made in seconding the nomination. [Cries of "no," etc.]

THE PRESIDENT—If I understand the delegate, the motion is, that two speeches may be made for each person nominated as Vice President, the one of ten minutes and the other of five minutes in support of same.

MR. COCHRANE, of New York—Mr. President, by order of the Convention, it has proceeded to the business of nominating the candidates, and nothing else is now in order until that is accomplished. [Cries of "Right!" "Good!"]

MR. McCLURE, of Pennsylvania—I suppose I could not reach it, properly, except by moving a suspension of the Rules.

THE PRESIDENT—The Chairman is of opinion that the Convention has control of the subject.

MR. McCLURE of Pennsylvania—I see that I cannot reach it without moving a suspension, and, therefore, I will withdraw the motion.

MR. BROWN, of Pennsylvania—Coming, as I do, from Pennsylvania, which desires to present a very popular and estimable gentleman to the office of Vice President, through a majority of her delegation—but coming, also, as I do, from the great county of Alleghany, a county which gave ten thousand majority for Abraham Lincoln, and which will give ten thousand again, in my estimation, for Schuyler Colfax—[great applause]—I desire, gentlemen of the Convention, to be distinctly understood that I speak for myself, and not for the delegation, or any part of the delegation.

Another Delegate—"That's so!"

Mr. Brown, of Pennsylvania—Yes, it is!

A Delegate—No; and no part of the State at all.

Mr. Brown—I have come from the county which gives the Republican majority in Pennsylvania.

A Voice—You pretend to represent it.

Mr. Brown, of Pennsylvania—I come from the county that gives more Republican majority than all the rest of the State put together. I believe that Schuyler Colfax is the choice of Alleghany county, and, speaking for myself, will vote for him first, last, and all the time.

Mr. McClure, of Pennsylvania—Mr. President—

Mr. Hassaurek, of Ohio—Mr. President—

Mr. McClure—I will withhold for the present.

OHIO NOMINATES BENJ. F. WADE FOR VICE PRESIEENT.

Mr. Hassaurek of Ohio—The Ohio delegation, Mr. President, instructed by the State Convention, and of their own unanimous choice, present for the Vice Presidency a name which has found a place in the hearts of every earnest Republican [applause]; the name of that veteran champion of freedom and human rights, the Hon. Benj. F. Wade. [Loud applause.] Mr. President, like the great and immortal Abraham Lincoln, Mr. Wade arose from the lower and humbler walks of life, a child of the people.

Like the great emancipator, Mr. Wade is a self-made man, who fought his early way through difficulties, poverty, and obscurity. And, Mr. President and gentlemen of the Convention, if we cherish the memory of Abraham Lincoln as the author of the proclamation of emancipation, we must not forget that Benjamin F. Wade, like John the Baptist of old, preceded him as a preacher in the wilderness. [Applause.] There is another resemblance, Mr. President, between Benjamin F. Wade and our martyred President; it is that incorruptible virtue for which the people have designated him by the name of "Honest Ben. Wade." [Applause.]

There is no man throughout the length and breadth of this land, be he Democrat or Republican, who doubts the honesty of Benjamin F. Wade. If there is one man at Washington who watches over the people's money, and opposes with unrelenting hostility all schemes of lobbyists and corruptionists, that man is Benjamin F. Wade. [Applause.] And, although, he does not always do it in the choicest and gentlest terms of polite language [laughter]; but sir, he does it in the language of indignant honesty and unpurchasable rectitude. [Applause.] He is entitled for his meritorious public services to the second highest gift at the hands of the nation. If the active, the positive, and the strong men of the party, are not to be deserted by their friends, then, gentlemen, this Convention will say to "Honest Ben. Wade," "well done, thou good and faithful servant."

MISSOURI SECONDS THE NOMINATION OF BENJ. F. WADE.

Mr. Schurz, of Missouri—Mr. President, I am instructed by a large majority of the delegation from the State of Missouri, to second the nomination just made. [Applause.] It has been properly suggested by the gentleman from Illinois (Mr. Palmer), to day, that the Republican party, in making a nomination for the office of President, ought to consider well one thing, that we present no temptations to the dagger of the assassin [applause]; and I am bold to say, that, if Ben. Wade is put behind Gen. Grant, there is not a Life Insurance Company in the world, that will not at once want to take a premium on the life of Gen. Grant. [Applause.] I need not speak of the career of the old chieftain. We all know that he is one of those men whom no flatterer can seduce, whom no threat can frighten, and no violence can coerce. [Applause.] Look at him now, as he stands in Washington, all the powers of corruption combined against him—and there he stands like a column of marble. [Applause.] I ask this Convention to stand by him.

OHIO SECONDS THE NOMINATION OF BENJ. F. WADE.

Mr. Spaulding, of Ohio—I wish to say, sir, that I have attended all the Republican Conventions, I think, since the organization of the Republican party, and I never yet knew the delegation of my own State united upon a candidate, never; but now, after eighteen years of experience of the "brave old Ben" in the Senate of the United States, Ohio stands here to give him forty-two. [Applause.] Sir, I need not speak further in commendation of our candidate, and I will not further take the time of the Convention.

NORTH CAROLINA SECONDS THE NOMINATION OF BENJ. F. WADE.

Mr. Jones, of North Carolina—Mr. President, representing the State of North Carolina, we have no candidate to present from that State; but North Carolina, in appreciation of the gallant services done the Republican party by that old Roman veteran, Ben. Wade [applause], has instructed her representatives, on this floor, to cast her votes for Ben. Wade. [Applause.] Mr. President, I do not desire to take up any of the time of this valuable Convention [laughter], but I will say to the great West, that I believe his nomination will give greater strength upon the ticket, than any other name that can be presented. [Applause.] Why, sir, in the Convention of North Carolina, that has recently presented a constitution to the people of North Carolina for its adoption, the candidates upon the respective State tickets have used this argument, sir, looking to the Congress of the United States as the means of removing that arch-traitor, Andrew Johnson, they have held out the inducement that old Ben. Wade would be in the Presidential chair, to aid in the great work of reconstruction that they have so much at heart. Every speaker that I know of, that has been on the stump in North Carolina, has pointed to Old Ben. Wade, as the man to mete out justice to them; and, sir, in conclusion, on behalf of the State, I say, we are ready to wade in. [Applause.]

NEW YORK NOMINATES REUBEN E. FENTON.

Mr. Tremaine, of New York—Mr. President—[Applause.]

The President—Judge Tremain, of New York, has the floor. [Applause.]

Mr. Tremain, of New York—In behalf of four hundred thousand Union Republicans in the Empire State, I have the honor to present to the Convention the name of New York's favorite son, Reuben E. Fenton. [Applause.] The public career of Mr. Fenton during the ten years that he held the office of Representative in Congress, and during the four years that he has so creditably filled the office of Chief Magistrate of our State, has rendered his name and fame familiar to every member of this Convention. He was one of the earliest and most prominent founders of the Republican party, and as early as 1855 presided over the first State Convention held by that young and vigorous political organization. [Applause.] He is emphatically a man of the people; sound and earnest in all his political views [applause]; with sagacity and prudence that preserved him from political mistakes; without a superior as an efficient and successful political organizer; he generally secures victory for those with whom he works, and is one who wields a commanding influence in the affairs of our State and nation. His unselfish support of the great cause of freedom and justice has been a marked trait in his character, and strikingly exemplified throughout his whole political career. When the rebellion broke out he threw himself into the cause of his country with all the ardor of his nature, and so conscientiously and carefully did he devote himself to the welfare and the interests of our brave boys in blue that he was everywhere hailed by the soldiers with the appellation of "Fenton, the soldiers' friend." [Applause.]

In 1862 the great States of New York, Pennsylvania and Ohio swung from their moorings, and temporarily abandoned the cause of that party which was straining every nerve to crush out the rebellion and uphold the honor and integrity of the nation. It was a grievous error, and grievously have the people suffered from it. For two bitter years New York suffered under the administration of Horatio Seymour, and when the hour came for deliverance her sons turned instinctively to Reuben E. Fenton to become their standard-bearer. He took the field, and, although Seymour was then in the zenith of his power and popularity, Reuben E. Fenton overthrew this Goliah of modern democracy, and was elected Governor of the State of New York by ten thousand majority. [Applause.] Two years afterward he came before the people, and, with a record made glorious by his course in the war, he was elected by a majority of over eight thousand. Two years afterward he was again nominated, by acclamation, for Governor, and, although his antagonist, the Mayor of New York, by reason of his official position, his residence, and his personal popularity, possessed extraordinary strength, Fenton was elected by an increased majority of fifteen thousand. [Applause.]

Sir—the question is a natural one—"Can you carry New York, with her thirty-three electoral votes, for Reuben E. Fenton?" I give you the answer, coming from the free and frank interchange of sentiment of sixty-six gentlemen, fresh from the people. The election of 1867 was no indication of the popular sentiment on the national issues; and, sir, there is no reason to believe that the people intended to reverse the judgment which they deliberately pronounced in 1866, when they triumphantly sustained the patriotic policy of reconstruction adopted by Congress.

Mr. Fenton was elected by fifteen thousand majority the last time he was before the people. We know, sir, that the naturalization process, aided by the dram shops of New York, are multiplying Democratic voters, but we shall overcome them by the increase in part of the young men who are rising in our land to vote with us, and by the force of sound religion and increasing morality.

While we believe that we shall carry New York for any candidate, it is our undoubted conviction that, with Grant and Fenton for our standard-bearers, we shall give a decisive majority to the nominee of this Convention. Sir, in the cruel war through which we have passed, New York made great sacrifices. She poured out her blood and treasure like water. She claims no credit for it. In the future, as in the past, under all circumstances, and at all hazards, she will, combining her merchant princes with her professional men, and all that are loyal, crush out all repudiation and maintain the plighted credit, honor and faith of the nation. [Great applause.]

Sir, if you concur in the opinion of the Republicans of New York, we shall not only appreciate the honor and the responsibility you have conferred, but the intelligence, which goes flashing over the wires communicating the result of your proceedings, will so inspire our constituents with a sense of gratitude, of determination, and of resolution, that they will enter upon the contest as irresistible as the charges of the "Old Guard" of Napoleon Bonaparte. [Applause.] When the result shall have been achieved and the victory shall have been won, then you will hear the powerful voice of New York joining with her loyal sister States in the grand national chorus, and she will be entitled to claim a proud share in the honor of the great and glorious victory that shall have been achieved. [Tremendous cheering.]

REMARKS OF MR. STORRS.

MR. STORRS, of Illinois—We remember well, when in 1864, the conflict we were then waging was transferred from the Potomac to the city of New York, the cohorts of the rebellion were under the command of Horatio Seymour, and the people of this nation were as much interested, and its future existence as vitally depended upon the success of that contest, as it did, sir, upon the contest being waged before Richmond. I have not forgotten, and the people of this nation have not forgotten, that our leader in that great contest in the State of New York, was Reuben E. Fenton, of that State. [Great Cheers.] I have not forgotten, sir, and I cannot forget while I remember the glories of our country, that, organizing the true and loyal men of our nation, he drove sedition out of the City and State of New York, and placed the glory of victory again upon our banner. Two years ago, sir, our battles were re-fought. I have not forgotten, that all the powers of an unscrupulous party, aided by more unscrupulous apostates [cheers], were again enlisted against the Republican organization. Sir, apostates do not flourish well upon the soil of the West; and, if there is any State above all others whose loyalty caused the people of the West to rejoice, it was the State of New York when we saw the followers of Johnson borne down under inevitable defeat, by an army led by Reuben E. Fenton, of New York. Sir, "Peace hath her victories, not less renowned than war."

We have put the great military captain of the age at the head of one ticket, and I, sir, in seconding the motion of the gentleman from New York, propose that the great civil chieftain of the Empire State, be second upon the ticket. I second the nomination. [Great cheering.]

MR. LOGAN, of Illinois—I did not intend, sir, to say one word in reference to the candidates presented for the Vice Presidency, nor do I desire now, sir, to descant on the qualifications or the merits of either of the candidates. They are all good men; they are all loyal and capable; but if I should sit still, as Chairman of the Illinois delegation, after the remarks of one of the delegates, it might be understood that he represented the entire delegation. I merely rise to say, that, I will announce that Illinois stands fifteen votes for Benjamin F. Wade [cheers], eleven votes for Hannibal Hamlin [applause], three votes for Schuyler Colfax [cheers], and three votes for Reuben E. Fenton. [Cheers.]

LOUISIANA SECONDS THE NOMINATION OF R. E. FENTON.

MR. WARMOTH, of Louisiana—I rise, sir, simply for the purpose of stating that the delegation from Louisiana instruct me to second the nomination of Gov. Fenton, of New York. [Great cheering.]

KENTUCKY NOMINATES JAMES SPEED FOR VICE PRESIDENT.

MR. WOOD, of Kentucky—Mr. Chairman, the delegation from the State of Kentucky, have instructed me to present the name of Hon. James Speed, for the office of Vice President. [Cheers.] In presenting the name of Mr. Speed, I am proud to say, that he is not unknown to the American people. During the darkest days of this Republic; during the rebellion, when everything seemed to threaten the overthrow of the government, Mr. Speed, at the earliest possible period, took his place in the Union Republican party, and under that banner he has ever fought. [Applause.] There is no man in this Union, who stands higher in the State of Kentucky, than Mr. Speed. Mr. Speed, sir, was the confidential friend and adviser of the late lamented Mr. Lincoln. He was a member, as is well known to this Convention, of Mr. Lincoln's Cabinet, and was conspicuous for his great ability, and for his incorruptible integrity. He remained in the Cabinet of Mr. Lincoln, as is well known, and remained in that Cabinet until some time after Mr. Johnson assumed control of the government.

THE PRESIDENT—The Chair is obliged to call for order. It is with very great difficulty that Mr. Wood can be heard.

MR. WOOD, of Kentucky—Mr. Lincoln, who well knew Mr. Speed, and who knew his sterling character, his incorruptible integrity, and his moral worth, selected him as a member of his Cabinet. He remained in that Cabinet until after Mr. Lincoln's assassination, and after Mr. Johnson's inauguration to the Presidency. He remained in Mr. Johnson's Cabinet, until Mr. Johnson proved himself a traitor to the Republican party. When Mr. Speed found that there was no opportunity to be useful in that Cabinet, he, like a proud and noble man, retired from that Cabinet into private life, and is now exerting his great talents and influence for the Republican party. If Mr. Speed should receive the nomination of this Convention, there is no man in this broad Union, who can exert a more powerful influence on the success of that party. Kentucky will give her undivided support to him, and we trust that all loyal men throughout the Union will do the same.

MARYLAND NOMINATES J. A. J. CRESSWELL FOR VICE PRESIDENT.

Mr. Sands, of Maryland—Mr. President, after the names, world-wide known, that have been placed before this Convention, and after the applause which has greeted the mention of these names, the task which I have to perform, which is laid upon me by my State, is somewhat difficult. It might seem, sir, that my associates and myself, coming from a State bound hand andfoot, to day, by the treachery of a recreant President, and a recreant Governor who is too mean to have his name breathed here to day—it might seem that we should be quiet. But, sir, though we are to day at the mercy of treason, I tell to you, that within the limits of that State, there are fifty thousand knees that have never bowed to the Baal of treason. [Applause.] When, in 1861, the fires of patriotism were attempted to be extinguished, they went out to the valleys and hills, and kindled them there, and, please God, we will keep them there, as long as there is a single hand to tend them. [Cheers.] In that year which took from us the beloved Abraham Lincoln—in that same year, God took from our little State, a man whose name was only second in our hearts to Lincoln —Henry Winter Davis. [Loud cheering.] Sir, as we watched his ascending spirit, we thought at last that we saw the man upon whom his mantle fell. We took him. We made him our representative; first, before the people in the forum, next, in the house of Representatives, and next in the Senate of the United States; and his vote, thank God, was the first of a majority which passed through the caucus of the Republican party of the United States—the first vote there for impartial suffrage. [Applause.] We honor him; Maryland honors him; and the men of Maryland, whose hearts are true to the nation, true to liberty, and true to impartial justice, sent us here to name him in this body, as her best beloved of to-day, and to put his name in nomination as a candidate for Vice President of the United States. I name him and have done—the Hon. John A. J. Cresswell, of Maryland.

REMARKS OF MR. TAYLOR.

Mr. Taylor, of Kentucky—I rise, sir, in behalf of the Kentucky delegation, to second the nomination of James Speed, of Kentucky. Gen. Speed has been from his boyhood a favorite son of that State. Gen. Speed has been from his infancy to manhood, a friend of human rights; from his boyhood to his manhood, he was anti-slavery, and as far back as 1859, in the State of Kentucky, when it was necessary for a man of stern manhood and integrity, to get up and vindicate his principles; even as far back as 1849, he advocated then a change in the constitution, and he was a candidate before the people, for the purpose of emancipating the slaves of the State of Kentucky. From that time to the present, he has followed that same career. He has never yielded with a truckling spirit to the pro-slavery party. He has preserved his manhood to so great an extent, that when Abraham Lincoln became the President of the United States, in the first year of his administration, he called him to the Cabinet as one of his advisers.

THE PRESIDENT—The Chair regrets to be again obliged to call for better order. It is simple justice to the gentleman from Kentucky. If any persons are obliged to leave the hall, let them do so quietly. Proceed!

MR. TAYLOR, of Kentucky—He continued in the discharge of his duties at the National Capital, until he could no longer participate in the counsels of Johnson, without compromising his manhood, and, true to his patriotic impulses, he withdrew from that council, and returned to private life. [Applause.] I cannot come before you to-day, pledging you the vote of Kentucky at the next Presidential election, but I can come before you, my countrymen, and pledge to you a candidate, who is true to all his principles of Republicanism, who will never betray the principles upon which the Republican party stands; and who has no impulse in his heart, that does not beat in unison with the great Republican party of the country.

REMARKS OF MR. CRESSWELL.

MR. CRESSWELL, of Maryland—I ask the indulgence of the Convention for a moment to explain somewhat the singular position that I occupy upon this floor. My name having been mentioned in connection with the high office, the nomination for which is your present business, it is incumbent on me to say what I am about to say. It is true that the State Convention of my own State, actuated by a desire to compliment me, complimented me by instructing my associates to cast for me their first ballot. I have requested that the delegation forego the compliment. They have as peremptorily declined. Under the circumstances, therefore, I am obliged to acquiesce, but preserve, however, a right to direct one vote which is under my control. I shall vote from a high sense of duty.

If I had the privilege of complimenting all the gentlemen who have been named, I should be obliged to vote for them all. I have the pleasure of a personal acquaintance with each of them. I know them all to be true and faithful Republicans. But, in this emergency—in this time when all the Republican party have at stake is in the issue—at this juncture of affairs, I believe it my duty to give my vote for the man whose life has contributed so much to the establishment of the principles of Republicanism,—I mean glorious old Ben. Wade, of Ohio. [Applause.] I have seen that old veteran in the midst of the storm of battle, and I know that he has never been shaken in his purpose. He stands for the right, without fear and without reproach, and he stands before the people of the United States, to-day, more than any other man, as an exponent of the principles which we seek to make immortal in the grand contest in the coming presidential conflict. One more treason may strike them down; one more victory makes the eternal truths which we have proclaimed, and which we have fought for in our battles. I can, truthfully, cast my vote to sustain the old veteran with his sturdy frame covered all over with the glittering insignia of illustrious achievements in behalf of his party. [Cheers.]

PENNSYLVANIA NOMINATES A. G. CURTIN, FOR VICE PRESIDENT.

MR. FORNEY, of Pennsylvania—Mr. President, as Chairman of the Republican State Delegation of Pennsylvania, I have the honor to nominate Andrew Gregg Curtin as the Republican candidate for Vice President. [Loud cheers.] I deeply regret my own condition, and that it prevents me from speaking of this distinguished citizen as he deserves, and as I desire to speak. I, therefore, devolve the duty upon Mr. McClure. [Applause.]

MR. MCCLURE, of Pennsylvania—Mr. President and Gentlemen of the Convention, I rise, not to speak for Andrew G. Curtin. He needs not the Vice Presidency of the United States to increase his fame, nor to increase the affection of his people for him. I rise not to tell the story of his official career. That is known as well in Chicago as in Pennsylvania; as well upon the shores of the Pacific as upon the shores of his own Atlantic. I arise to speak in behalf of the three hundred thousand Republicans of Pennsylvania, who stand charged in the contest with carrying the very centre of the enemy's column, and giving success to our great cause in November. [Applause.]

I say I speak not for men, nor do I speak from State pride. I appeal to the delegates of this Convention, in the words of truth and soberness, asking them to bear well in mind that as Pennsylvania shall cast her vote on the second Tuesday of October, so, in all human probability, shall the verdict of this great nation be rendered in November. I ask the members of this Convention to bear well in mind that after we shall have entered into this great national struggle for freedom—for a final victory—for the logical consequences of the war—that every loyal heart throughout this entire nation will turn, with quickened emotion, to the Keystone State in October; that every loyal eye will turn with steady gaze upon the verdict of her people, and that, if she shall declare in behalf of the policy and principles of the Republican party, then your victory is complete—your great battle is won.

I present, in behalf of Pennsylvania, to this Convention the name of Andrew G. Curtin, solely as the precursor of success in this contest. [Applause.] And I need not say that I do not present a man in any sense unworthy of the distinguished compliment we ask this Convention to give him. In 1860, when they turned to Illinois and took her favorite son for the Presidency, I know well (for I bore some humble part in that contest) how Pennsylvania determined it for Illinois, determined it for New York, determined it for New Jersey, determined it for the Union, by her majority of thirty-two thousand for Andrew G. Curtin. [Cheers.]

We selected him with reference to the great issues, as well as with reference to the great national success. We knew that upon us devolved the duty of carrying the stronghold of the enemy's works. We selected the man most fitting, the man the most worthy, the man strongest in the hearts and the affections of the people of Pennsylvania. And by his matchless eloquence, and by his brilliant leadership, she gave her first verdict squarely for the Republican party in 1860, and gave her sixty thousand for Lincoln in November. And I remember well, too, in our State, when gloom prevailed throughout the Union; when loyal heads were bowed in despair; when men felt almost on the verge of disaster; when Indiana fell, and Iowa swerved; when New York gave her Seymour, and New Jersey her Parker; and in the first great contest to redeem what we had won in 1860 and lost, we called him again because he was of all men the man most fitted to the occasion, of all men the most powerful. In 1863, the country having advanced, having learned in the school of war that we must plant our banner forward, and march onward, we again turned to Andrew G. Curtin, of Pennsylvania, and charged him with the duty of saving the State, and saving the common country.

THE PRESIDENT—Gentlemen of the Convention, the gentleman's time is exhausted. Shall more time be given him?

Cries—"Go on! go on!"

THE PRESIDENT—I made the suggestion, because Colonel Forney, who made the nomination, is unable to speak and present the claims of that candidate.

MR. MCCLURE, of Pennsylvania—I say, in 1863, when almost every loyal heart was stricken in despair, when our most faithful States seemed to have wavered in their fidelity, and when we had to commence the great work and turn back this tide of disaster, Pennsylvania then sought for her most trusted, her most honored, her most successful leader, and Andrew G. Curtin was again made our standard-bearer. Then, as now, he had been so eminent in good deeds, as to have ignoble foes. But he took the banner of emancipation [cheers], and bore it in triumph in Pennsylvania from the Lakes to the Delaware. He rallied around it the faithful people of our Commonwealth, as no other man could rally it then, or can rally it now [cheers]; and, with seventy thousand of our noble soldiers in the field, disfranchised by a court faithless to the cause of our country, he was again triumphantly elected by a majority of fifteen thousand votes, and Pennsylvania was saved, and your nation was saved. [Renewed cheers.] I need not say that he is pre-eminent in our State, because he is known everywhere the same, as the soldier's friend, and the great civilian hero of the war. [Cheers.]

I dispute not the eminent merits of the distinguished civilian presented by New York; but I say if there is one man who towers over all others as the great civilian hero of this war, it is Andrew G. Curtin, of Pennsylvania. [Applause.] There is Pennsylvania, gentlemen of the Chicago convention! There is Pennsylvania! Behold her! He has made her record during this war. He has written her history during this war. He has advanced her every step she has advanced, for freedom, for justice, and for liberty and for law. I need not refer to him. I refer to our State, because the history of our State for the last six years is the history of Andrew G. Curtin. There is not a soldier's home where his name is not lisped in love throughout our great commonwealth, and wherever there is a grave of our martyred soldiers, and where they sleep in every valley, there is not a tomb of a martyr so humble, there is not an altar where his name is not lisped with reverence and affection. I appeal to this Convention—not for him, not for my State. I appeal to this Convention in behalf of the millions of Republicans of the Union—in behalf of victory. I do not say, gentlemen, that we shall be faithless if any other candidate is presented. Far from it. Pennsylvania has been too often tried, too often trusted, and has manifested her fidelity under every circumstance; and whatever may be the choice of this Convention, she will give her united, earnest, and, I trust, successful efforts for the nominee. [Cheers and prolonged applause.]

THE PRESIDENT—The gentleman's time has expired.

IOWA NOMINATES JAMES HARLAN FOR VICE PRESIDENT.

MR. WILLIAMSON, of Iowa—Mr. President, I am instructed, by the delegation from Iowa, to place in nomination for the office of Vice President of the United States, the name of one of Iowa's most favored public men [laughter], the name of a man whose public life and career has been a synonym for that of purity and political fidelity—the name of a man who resigned the high office of cabinet minister when he could no longer find friends of the country, of the constitution, and of the people with whom to consult in that high position. It is only necessary for me to mention the name of the Hon. James Harlan, United States Senator from Iowa [cheers]; a man whose whole life has been devoted to the principles of justice, who has stood firm and fast by the great principles of the party, when others, whom we have equally trusted, have deceived and ignored the express wishes of the people of the State and of the United States. [A voice—"Grimes!"]

It is not necessary to make any extended remarks, as the gentlemen calling out the name of Mr. Grimes on so many occasions bring the mantling blush of shame to any speaker who is not in the habit of addressing large assemblages of this kind. [Applause and laughter.]

SOUTH CAROLINA SECONDS THE NOMINATION OF HENRY WILSON.

MR. WHITMORE, of South Carolina—Mr. President and Gentlemen of the Convention: No other emotion save that which is the proudest and the noblest, can inspire the hearts of those who are the representatives of the people, here to-day. When the names of each of the noblest sons of the country, most experienced in statesmanship, are brought before us, and we are called upon by the eloquence of the gentlemen who present them, our sympathies are stirred within us. I have nothing to say against the claims of any of the gentlemen who have been presented for our consideration. I trust, however, that our hearts may be animated with the purest desire to protect the rights and privileges and grand principles of our party, in the nomination which we shall make for the Vice Presidency of the United States. It may seem strange, Mr. President and Gentlemen, that South Carolina with her voice here to day, in behalf of one hundred thousand voters—South Carolina, with principles so antipodean in the past to the sentiments of the platform which has been adopted here to day—should stand here, in this hour, to give her voice in favor of one of Massachusetts' proudest sons. [Great applause.] We wear, Mr. President and Gentlemen of this Convention, his name upon our badges, and the remembrance of his deeds, and the great duties which he has fulfilled, in our hearts. We stand here well men, true and strong, representing the Republicans of South Carolina, to throw our voice and vote into the scale in preference of Hon. Henry Wilson, of Massachusetts. [Applause.]

REMARKS OF MR. KELFER.

MR. KELFER, of Alabama—Mr. President and Gentlemen of the Convention—It may seem improper, perhaps, in a representative from Alabama to add yet another name to the already long list of acceptable men, for any one of whom the whole Republican party of this country may well be proud to give their suffrages; and yet, Mr. President, the poor step-children of the Union in Alabama—[laughter]—that State whose name means "Here we rest," and where we Republicans have no rest, so far as we can see, are hardly likely to have [laughter]—still, Mr. President, we feel that a debt of gratitude requires on the part of some of us standing here as delegates of the Republican party of that State to recognize, if we can, even by a few votes, the sentiment of gratitude that we feel for one whose name is cherished in the State of Alabama, second to none of the illustrious men who have been named heretofore in connection with this high office. I mean to name, sir, for Vice President, the Hon. William D. Kelley, of Pennsylvania. [Applause and laughter.] Gentlemen may laugh if they please, Mr. President, but we all know in the coming campaign there is no man in these United States whose clarion voice will bring voters up to the work before them, in a manner to surpass that in which they will be brought by William D. Kelley. [Laughter.] And if there is a doubtful Congressional District, who do they send for to canvass it but William D. Kelley, of Pennsylvania? [Cheers.] He is the man whom we want to marshal our voters to the polls. He is a man on whom the mantle of Henry Clay, as the great champion of American industry, has fallen. He is the champion of the rights of the laboring men everywhere. He has been the life-long devoted friend of human liberty and equal rights. And we of the South never appeal to him in vain for advice, counsel, and assistance, when it has been denied by many to whom, perhaps, the gentlemen might think it more advisable to give their votes at this time. We feel a debt of gratitude to Judge Kelley, and, although his claims have not been brought forward prominently as a candidate in this Convention, some of us, at least, will recognize the debt we owe him by our votes on this occasion.

REMARKS OF MR. SEYMOUR.

Mr. Seymour, of Wisconsin—I wish to declare, sir, that in rising to mention and propose the name of Hannibal Hamlin, of Maine, [applause,] that I have not arrogated to myself the honor or the pleasure of expressing the wishes of the Wisconsin delegation. The Wisconsin delegation is divided, by giving Colfax eleven, Fenton six, Hamlin two, and Curtin one. [Applause.] I merely, sir, rise in the name of those who desire to vote for this honored man, that the name should be put in nomination. This candidate is a man who is a head and shoulders above all corrupting influences. We do not wish to charge one word of objection upon any gentleman that is named; not even to intimate their unfitness. On the contrary, the multiplicity and respectability of the candidates afford abundance of evidence that the Republican party is full of good material for the Vice Presidency. But we know that we must, in this campaign, consolidate and organize all the Union element of the nation, and we think this nomination will do it. There is nothing that will put the Republican party in a state of invincibility so much as to go back and correct the blunder that was made at Baltimore, in 1864. It will be regarded by the people as a pledge of the Republican party to a return to soundness; it would re-light the campaign fires, and, with the enthusiasm of 1860, the party of Lincoln and Hamlin would again unite and march on to victory. He is one of the few public men in this country upon whose name the politicians have never been able to throw a stain. [Cheers.] He is respected at home and abroad as a man of unsullied character, as a man true to the principles of the Republican party—true to the interests of the United States. [Applause.]

MAINE NOMINATES HANNIBAL HAMLIN, OF MAINE, FOR VICE PRESIDENT.

Mr. Shepley, of Maine—Mr. President, instructed by the delegates, who are themselves instructed by the people of Maine, I rise to lay before you, on behalf of the Republicans of Maine, and on behalf of those whose hearts respond to the memories of the old ticket of "Lincoln and Hamlin" [cheers]—to nominate Hannibal Hamlin, of Maine. [Cheers.] Four years ago, the National Republican Convention laid aside a candidate who had been tried and found true and faithful, to take up a candidate whom the representatives of the people have been obliged to put upon trial, for high crimes and misdemeanors [cheers], and against whom the unanimous voice of the loyal people of the country has pronounced the verdict of guilty [Cheers.] The mistake of that day—the mistake of that hour, has cost us, and is costing us, to-day, through the treachery of Andrew Johnson, thousands and tens of thousands of lives of loyal men in the South. It cost us the life of Abraham Lincoln [sensation], and, unless the official guillotine be soon set to work, it may cost us the life of the nation.

I will not go further into the history of those mistakes, but there would seem to be a poetical justice, now, in retracing our steps, and presenting to the people of this country the associated names from Illinois and from Maine, as on the old ticket of "Lincoln and Hamlin." [Cheers.] It would be a ticket, glorious with all the memories and associations of the past. [Cheers.] It would be a ticket, radiant with every promise of victory and security for the future. I am not going into a biography of the candidate whom we represent. The golden page of history, which records the highest advancement in human freedom and human progress, is illuminated in golden letters with the names of Lincoln and Hamlin. [Applause.] His record is before the country. He has been tried and proved, and has not been found wanting. We do not ask you to nominate him as a compliment to Hannibal Hamlin. He has once received that token of the nation's appreciation. We do not ask you to nominate Hannibal Hamlin as necessary to carry the State of Maine. We will give you our vote for any candidate whom you may name in this Convention. [Cheers.] We do say, however, if you do give us the name of Hannibal Hamlin on this ticket, that as we are the first State, almost, to record our vote in the coming campaign, we will pitch the key-note, with Grant and Hamlin on the ticket, and we will pitch it so high that no discordant sound of treason shall ever be heard. [Applause.]

REMARKS OF MR. SOUTHER.

Mr. Souther, of Pennsylvania—I only get up to say, Mr. President, that, as the name of another individual from Pennsylvania has been presented here, and no one seconds that nomination, I simply rise to say that I do not second it—that I was sent here for a different purpose—that the delegation from Pennsylvania came here under instructions to vote for A. G. Curtin. That is what they came here for that is what they were commanded to do; and, perhaps, I should not have troubled this Convention for one moment were it not for the fact that, throughout this city, ever since the delegates came here, it has been told that Andrew G. Curtin was not the choice of Pennsylvania, and that there was opposition to him in our own Convention. That opposition has manifested itself here this mornng, and it amounts to about the same thing as the man's interest in the oil well, which was one thirty-second of one forty-second, and it was a dry hole! [Laughter.] I can only say, sir, that we have presented the name of Andrew G. Curtin here in good faith, as has been well said here by the gentleman who seconded the nomination.

There is some part of this contest to be fought in Pennsylvania, and I will only say that during the war all eyes were at one time turned to Pennsylvania, on the eve of a battle, and her conduct on that day was considered to be the turning point in the struggle. It may, perhaps, be so in this contest, and we have, therefore, made a choice which gives no uncertain or doubtful sound. We can certainly tell what will become of Pennsylvania. We ask you, gentlemen, to take this matter to your serious consideration, and, if we are not favored with our candidate, we will simply say that we came instructed by the State Convention to present the name of Andrew G. Curtin, as the unanimous choice of Pennsylvania.

REMARKS OF MR. HUMPHREY.

Mr. Humphrey, of Alabama—Mr. President, without solicitation, or, at least, without any authority from the delegation of Alabama as a delegation, one of our delegates, from personal consideration, from the high regard and respect which he has for Judge Kelley, presented his name. It is the presentation of but one man of the delegation, and whilst the delegation from Alabama has the highest regard and respect for the statesmanship of Mr. Kelley, for the statesmanship of Mr. Wade, of Mr. Colfax, and of the other gentlemen whose names have been mentioned in connection with the Vice Presidency, we feel, Mr. President, that so far as the State of Alabama is concerned, her destiny depends upon the exactest statesmanship that can be administered in the affairs of the Government for the next coming years. And, sir, with a view not to disparage any one, nor with a view to enter into a fulsome eulogy upon any individual, I shall mention a name which understands and comprehends, as we conceive, the great issues which are involved in the reconstruction policy. Sir, although the delegation will be divided, there will be a respectable vote given for the man. I mention the Hon. Henry Wilson, of Massachusetts.

REMARKS OF MR. RASTER.

Mr. Raster, of Illinois—Mr. President, eleven delegates of the State of Illinois second the nomination of that man, whose name is inseparably connected with the most glorious page in the history of the Republican party—the name of the Hon. Hannibal Hamlin, of Maine. [Applause.] In going back in our memories to the history of our party, we would not willingly rest upon the recollections of 1864. But we do like to return to the year 1860, as the year of our triumph. In the platform that has been adopted, to-day, we have a bill of indictment, as it were, of the nation against Andrew Johnson. That indictment has been applauded by this Convention. But has it not occurred to you that it was by the Republican party Johnson was placed in a position whence the weapon of an assassin raised him to the Presidency? We say, in our platform, that we regret having done so. But, sir, is that enough? Faith, without acts, is nothing; neither is confession without, penitence. The Republican party sinned, in 1864; it is now confessing that sin. We said, in 1864, that it was not good to swap horses in the middle of a stream; and yet we *did* swap one horse of the noble team which had carried us to victory. [Applause.] I take it that our platform will not be complete if, to the confession, we do not add the penitence. [Applause and laughter.] The error we did commit was greater, perhaps, than any one here would be willing to think of. Would our martyred President be a martyred President to-day if we had not swapped horses? What was said of honest Ben Wade, that he would be a shield to the life of General Grant, is true; but it was as true of the Hon. Hannibal Hamlin, in 1864, in regard to the life of the favorite son of Illinois. In that respect, and because we think that the best memories of the party would be revived by the name of Hannibal Hamlin, we second the nomination. But, at the same time, we have one other reason. It is this: There is as wide a discrepancy in regard to the Vice Presidency as there ever was in the selection of a candidate for the Presidency. A great number of men—good and true—have been nominated. I have not a single word to say against any one of them, and would not if I could; but I do say that, if there should be no union possible upon either one of the candidates named, I think that Hannibal Hamlin would be just the man to unite the friends of all the other candidates who have been nominated to-day. [Applause.]

MR. HUBBARD, of West Virginia—Mr. Chairman, Western Virginia desires that a vote shall be taken, in order that we may show our hands for the man we are in favor of. [Loud cheers, and cries of "Good! "good!"]

MR. ———, of Pennsylvania—Mr. President, I move you now, sir, that the nominations be closed, and that we proceed to vote; upon which I move the previous question.

[Cries of "no! no!"]

THE PRESIDENT—The Chair can not entertain the motion.

KANSAS NOMINATES S. C. POMEROY FOR VICE PRESIDENT.

MR. MARTIN, of Kansas—I simply desire to present the name of the honored and trusted citizen of our State: I submit as a candidate for the office of Vice President, the name of Senator Pomeroy, of Kansas. [Cheers.]

REMARKS OF GEN. SICKLES.

Mr. Sickles, of New York—Mr. President, I need not, perhaps, say anything in addition to what has already been said. Language would fail me in this hour, to add anything to the discussion we have heard, in regard to the candidates for the Vice Presidency; but I feel, sir, that I might do injustice to my own State, if I omitted to respond to the invitation extended to me by my own delegation, and the remarks made by my colleague in presenting the name of Governor Fenton, of New York. [Great applause.] The Convention of the Republican party of New York, in making its choice for the Vice Presidency, did not fail to give candid consideration to the services and qualifications of the statesmen of sister States. They thought, sir, that it was eminently proper—and in this they concurred with the views already presented here from other States—they thought it eminently proper, that the choice of this Convention for the Vice Presidency should fall upon one of the most eminent and able of the War Governors, who sustained our illustrious War Minister, Edwin M. Stanton. [Cheers and applause.] In that group of War Governors, we find a Curtin, of Pennsylvania; a Buckingham, of Connecticut; a Salomon, of Wisconsin; a Morton, of Indiana [applause]; the lamented Andrew, of Massachusetts [applause]; and last, not least, Reuben E. Fenton, of New York. [Applause.] There are many others. I cannot name them all. [Cheers.] If the Convention will make its choice from these—and we doubt not it will—we are sure it will not fail to meet the wishes of the people, and that the choice will fulfill the expectations of the loyal masses of the people of the United States. But, sir, let me say, that it seems to me nothing can be more fit, in the Presidential contest, than to have, as the lieutenant of the General who never lost a battle, a leader who never lost an election. [Cheers.]

The President—Gentlemen, the Convention informally indicates a desire for the roll call. Shall the roll be called?

Mr. Nowlan, of West Virginia—I move nominations be closed. ["No! no!"]

The President—By general consent, the Secretary will proceed to call the roll of States.

The Secretary then proceeded to call the roll of States, and announced the following result:

FIRST BALLOT.

STATES.	Wilson.	Colfax.	Wade.	Fenton.	Hamlin.	Curtin.	Harlan.	Pomeroy	Kelley	Speed.	Creswell
Alabama	4	4	2	2					4		
Arkansas	9		1								
California	1	2	5	2							
Colorado		6									
Connecticut	4	2	2	4							
Dakota		2									
Delaware	6										
District of Columbia			2								
Florida	2	2		2							
Georgia	6	2	3	6		1					
Idaho				2							
Illinois		3	15	3	11						
Indiana		26									
Iowa							16				
Kansas								6			
Kentucky										22	
Louisiana				14							
Maine					14						
Maryland			1								13
Massachusetts	24										
Michigan		16									
Minnesota			8								
Mississippi	5		5	4							
Missouri		2	20								
Montana			2								
Nebraska			6								
Nevada			2	4							
New Hampshire	10										
New Jersey		14									
New York				66							
North Carolina			18								
Ohio			42								
Oregon		6									
Pennsylvania		1	3			48					
Rhode Island	2	3	2		1						
South Carolina	12										
Tennessee		6	3	11							
Texas	11		1								
Vermont		10									
Virginia	18		2								
West Virginia	5	1	2			1					
Wisconsin		7		6	2	1					1
Total	119	115	147	126	28	51	16	6	4	22	14

THE PRESIDENT—Does the Convention desire the vote read for correction, or is the summary enough?

SEVERAL DELEGATES—The summary!

THE PRESIDENT—Gentlemen of the Convention, I read the statement of the vote:

The total number of votes cast is	648
Necessary to a choice	325
Mr. Wade has	147
Mr. Fenton has	126
Mr. Wilson has	119
Mr. Colfax has	115
Mr. Curtin has	51
Mr. Hamlin has	28
Mr. Speed has	22
Mr. Harlan has	16
Mr. Creswell has	14
Mr. Pomeroy has	6
Mr. Kelley has	4

You have made no choice. Is it your pleasure to proceed to another call of the roll?

VOICES—"Vote!" "Adjourn!" etc.

THE PRESIDENT—The Secretary will immediately proceed to another call of the roll. [Voices, "Adjourn!" "Vote!" etc.]

A DELEGATE from North Carolina—I move an adjournment until 7 o'clock this evening. [Cries of "No!" "Vote!" "Call the roll!"]

THE PRESIDENT—It seems to be the desire of the Convention to proceed to another call of the roll without any withdrawal of nominations.

MR ——— of North Carolina—I move an adjournment. [Cries of "No! go on with the vote!"

THE PRESIDENT—The Secretary will proceed to call the roll.

MR. WOOD, of Kentucky—On behalf of the delegation from Kentucky, I withdraw the name of Mr. Speed.

The Secretary then proceeded to call the roll of States upon a second ballot, with the following result:

SECOND BALLOT.

STATES.	Wilson.	Colfax.	Wade.	Fenton.	Hamlin.	Curtin.
Alabama	11	1	2	2	......	.....
Arkansas	10	......	......	......	......	.....
California	1	2	5	2	......	.....
Colorado	......	6	......	......	......	.....
Connecticut	4	1	3	4	......	.....
Dakota	......	2	......	......	......	.....
Delaware	......	5	......	......	......	1
District of Columbia	......	......	2	......	......	.....
Florida	2	2	......	2	......	.....
Georgia	2	2	7	7	......	.....
Idaho	......	......	......	2	......	.....
Illinois	......	3	15	3	11	.....
Indiana	......	26	......	......	......	.....
Iowa	......	4	......	10	2	.....
Kansas	......	2	2	2	......	.....
Kentucky	......	9	13	......	......	.....
Louisiana	......	......	......	14	......	.....
Maine	......	......	......	......	14	.....
Maryland	1	2	10	......	1	.....
Massachusetts	24	......	......	......	......	.....
Michigan	......	16	......	......	......	.....
Minnesota	......	......	8	......	......	.....
Mississippi	5	......	5	4	......	.....
Missouri	......	2	20	......	......	.....
Montana	......	......	2	......	......	.....
Nebraska	......	......	6	......	......	.....
Nevada	......	......	2	4	......	.....
New Hampshire	10	......	......	......	......	.....
New Jersey	......	14	......	......	......	.....
New York	......	......	......	66	......	.....
North Carolina	9	......	9	......	......	.....
Ohio	......	4	38	......	......	.....
Oregon	......	6	......	......	......	.....
Pennsylvania	......	3	5	......	......	44
Rhode Island	5	3	......	......	......	.....
South Carolina	12	......	......	......	......	.....
Tenessee	......	6	3	11	......	.....
Texas	......	......	9	3	......	.....
Vermont	......	10	......	......	......	.....
Virginia	12	4	2	2	......	.....
West Virginia	6	3	1	......	......	.....
Wisconsin	......	7	1	6	2	.....
Total	114	145	170	144	30	45

THE PRESIDENT—Gentlemen of the Convention, I read the statement of the vote:

Total number of votes cast	648
Necessary to a choice	325
Mr. Wade has	170
Mr. Colfax has	145
Mr. Fenton has	144
Mr. Wilson has	114
Mr. Curtin has	45
Mr. Hamlin has	30

Gentlemen of the Convention, you have made no choice. Will the Secretary proceed with the call of the roll?

VOICES—The roll!

A DELEGATE from Virginia—I move you, sir, that we adjourn until 7 o'clock to-night. [Many voices, "No!"]

THE PRESIDENT—It would seem to be unnecessary to put the vote. The Secretary will proceed to call the roll.

The Secretary then proceeded to call the roll, with the following result:

THIRD BALLOT.

STATES.	Wilson.	Colfax.	Wade.	Fenton.	Hamlin.	Curtin.
Alabama	11	1	2	2	......	.....
Arkansas	10	......	......	......	......	.....
California	......	1	8	1	......	.....
Colorado	......	6	......	......	......	.....
Connecticut	......	3	2	7	......	.....
Dakota	......	2	......	......	......	.....
Delaware	......	5	......	1	......	.....
District of Columbia	......	......	2	......	......	.....
Florida	2	2	......	2	......	.....
Georgia	......	4	6	8	......	.....
Idaho	......	......	......	2	......	.....
Illinois	......	4	17	3	8	.....
Indiana	......	26	......	......	......	.....
Iowa	......	8	......	8	......	.....
Kansas	......	2	2	2	......	.....
Kentucky	......	10	12	......	......	.....
Louisiana	......	......	5	9	......	.....
Maine	......	......	......	......	14	.....
Maryland	1	2	10	......	1	.....
Massachusetts	24	......	......	......	......	.....
Michigan	......	16	......	......	......	.....
Minnesota	1	......	7	......	......	.....
Mississippi	4	1	4	5	......	.....
Missouri	......	2	20	......	......	.....
Montana	......	......	2	......	......	.....
Nebraska	......	......	6	......	......	.....
Nevada	......	......	2	4	......	.....
New Hampshire	10	......	......	......	......	.....
New Jersey	......	14	......	......	......	.....
New York	......	......	......	66	......	.....
North Carolina	9	......	9	......	......	.....
Ohio	......	5	37	......	......	.....
Oregon	......	6	......	......	......	.....
Pennsylvania	......	5	7	......	......	40
Rhode Island	......	8	......	......	......	.....
South Carolina	12	......	......	......	......	.....
Tennessee	......	6	3	11	......	.....
Texas	......	......	11	1	......	.....
Vermont	......	10	......	......	......	.....
Virginia	10	6	2	2	......	.....
West Virginia	7	2	1	......	......	.....
Wisconsin	......	8	1	5	2	.....
Total	101	165	178	139	25	40

THE PRESIDENT—Gentlemen of the Convention, I read the statement of the vote:

Total number of votes cast....648
Necessary for a choice....325
Mr. Wade has....178
Mr. Colfax has....165
Mr. Fenton has....139
Mr. Wilson has....101
Mr. Curtin has.... 40
Mr. Hamlin has.... 25

MR. MCCLURE, of Pennsylvania—Mr. President— [Cries of "Vote!"]

THE PRESIDENT—The Chair must hear the gentleman from Pennsylvania. He has the floor.

MR. MCCLURE, of Pennsylvania—I hold in my hand a letter from Governor Curtin, of Pennsylvania, placed in the hands of the delegation. [Cries of "Louder!"]

I have in my hand a letter from Governor Curtin, addressed to the delegation from Pennsylvania, allowing them, in their discretion, to withdraw his name from this Convention. A majority of the delegation have instructed me now to present that letter, and thus withdraw his name from the Convention. Shall I read it? [Cries of "Read it! read it!"]

MR. MCCLURE, of Pennsylvania—Mr. President, I will read the letter.

"PHILADELPHIA, May 16, 1868.

"GENTLEMEN: While deeply sensible of the honor done me by the Republicans of Pennsylvania, in the cordial presentation of my name for the Vice Presidency, under the instructions of this Convention, directing the vote of the State to be cast for me, I do not feel justified, in this period of our country's peril, to allow my name to be used to embarrass, in any degree, the action of the delegation, in effecting what may be deemed best for the harmony of the party, and the success of our cherished principles. Never before in our history, was the success of loyal principles so vital to the peace and prosperity, and, indeed, the safety of the Republic, and no mere personal interest, or ambition, should be allowed to interfere with the deliberations of the people, or the declaration of their judgment. At the election, we must have the most cordial unity of action, and when my name stands in the way of it, the delegation should not hesitate to withdraw it from the list of candidates before the Convention. Fidelity to the harmony and interests of the Republican party will be the highest measure of fidelity to me, on the part of the Pennsylvania delegation. [Applause.] Appalling treachery, and emboldened treason, confront us, and the welfare of the living, and justice to the memory of the heroic dead, demand of all a singleness of purpose in making this last struggle for freedom, justice, and law. Do not hesitate to withdraw my name whenever, in your judgment, it will promote unity and harmony in the Republican party, and its ultimate triumph, which is so essential to the perpetuity of the government, and the prosperity and happiness of the American people.

"Very respectfully, your obedient servant,

"ANDREW G. CURTIN.

"*To the Pennsylvania Delegation in the National Republican Convention.*"

The Secretary then called the roll, with the following result:

FOURTH BALLOT.

STATES.	Wilson.	Colfax.	Wade.	Fenton.	Hamlin.
Alabama	11	1	2	2	.....
Arkansas	8	.....	2	.....	.....
California	.....	1	7	2	.....
Colorado	.....	6	.....	.....	.....
Connecticut	.....	2	2	8	.....
Delaware	.....	5	.....	1	.....
Dakota	.....	2	.....	.....	.....
Florida	2	2	.....	2	.....
District of Columbia	.....	.....	2	.....	.....
Georgia	.....	5	5	8	.....
Idaho	.....	.....	.....	2	.....
Illinois	.....	6	17	3	6
Indiana	.....	26	.....	.....	.....
Iowa	.....	8	.....	8	.....
Kansas	.....	2	2	2	.....
Kentucky	.....	10	12	.....	.....
Louisiana	.....	.....	5	9	.....
Maine	.....	.....	.....	.....	14
Maryland	1	3	10	.....	.....
Massachusetts	24	.....	.....	.....	.....
Michigan	.....	16	.....	.....	.....
Minnesota	1	.....	7	.....	.....
Mississippi	4	1	5	4	.....
Missouri	.....	2	20	.....	.....
Montana	.....	.....	2	.....	.....
Nebraska	.....	.....	6	.....	.....
Nevada	.....	.....	2	4	.....
New Hampshire	10	.....	.....	.....	.....
New Jersey	.....	14	.....	.....	.....
New York	.....	.....	.....	66	.....
North Carolina	7	.....	10	1	.....
Ohio	.....	6	36	.....	.....
Oregon	.....	6	.....	.....	.....
Pennsylvania	2	14	33	.....	3
Rhode Isiand	.....	6	2	.....	.....
South Carolina	7	.....	.....	5	.....
Tennessee	.....	6	3	11	.....
Texas	.....	1	11	.....	.....
Vermont	.....	10	.....	.....	.....
Virginia	5	10	2	3	.....
West Virginia	5	4	1	.....	.....
Wisconsin	.....	11	.....	3	2
Total	87	186	206	144	25

THE PRESIDENT—Gentlemen of the Convention, I read the statement of the vote:

Total number of votes cast....648
Necessary to a choice....325
Mr. Wade has....206
Mr. Colfax has....186
Mr. Fenton has....144
Mr. Wilson has.... 87
Mr. Hamlin has.... 25

Is it your pleasure to proceed to another ballot? [Cries of "Vote!"] The Secretary will proceed immediately to call the roll.

The Secretary then proceeded to call the roll on the fifth ballot, when the votes were cast as follows :

FIFTH BALLOT.

STATES.	Wade.	Colfax.	Fenton.	Hamlin.	Wilson.
Alabama	2	1	2		11
Arkansas	2				8
California	8	1	1		
Colorado		6			
Connecticut	2	4	6		
Dakota		2			
Delaware	2	4			
District of Columbia	2				
Florida		1	5		
Georgia	5	3	10		
Idaho			2		
Illinois	19	8	3	2	
Indiana		26			
Iowa		8	8		
Kansas	2	2	2		
Kentucky	12	10			
Louisiana	5		9		
Maine				14	
Maryland	10	3			1
Massachusetts					24
Michigan		16			
Minnesota	7				1
Mississippi	6	1	4		3
Missouri	20	2			
Montana	2				
Nebraska	6				
Nevada	1		5		
New Hampshire	9		1		
New Jersey		14			
New York			66		
North Carolina	9	7			2
Ohio	36	6			
Oregon		6			
Pennsylvania	20	30	1	1	
Rhode Island		8			
South Carolina	2		7		3
Tennessee	3	17			
Texas	12				
Vermont		10			
Virginia	2	10	5		3
West Virginia	1	9			
Wisconsin		11	2	3	
Total	207	226	139	20	56

Before the result of this ballot was announced, several delegations changed their votes.

MR. WILLIAMSON, of Iowa—Mr. President, Iowa desires to change the votes cast for Fenton to Colfax, and cast its entire sixteen votes for Colfax.

MR. MCCLURE, of Pennsylvania—Pennsylvania votes, sir, unanimously for Colfax. [Immense applause and great confusion, several gentlemen trying to obtain the floor.]

THE PRESIDENT—The Chair will not entertain any motion until there is better order. The gentleman from Louisiana first caught the eye of the Chair.

MR. WARMOUTH, of Louisiana—I am directed, sir, by the delegation from Louisiana to change its fourteen votes to Schuyler Colfax. [Applause.]

THE PRESIDENT—Gentlemen of the Convention, I am waiting to announce the gentleman from Connecticut, who is waiting to speak.

MR. BENT, of Connecticut—Mr. President, Connecticut desires to change her vote and make it unanimous for Schuyler Colfax. [Applause.]

MR. CLAFLIN, of Massachusetts—Mr. President, by authority of Senator Wilson, and by direction of the delegation from Massachusetts, I withdraw his name from this Convention, and Massachusetts desires her vote to be placed for Schuyler Colfax, of Indiana. [Applause and great confusion.]

THE PRESIDENT—The Chair will entertain no motion until there is better order, and will announce when he considers order restored.

MR. ———, of the District of Columbia—The District of Columbia, sir, desires to change its vote. [Applause.]

THE PRESIDENT—The gentleman will remain seated until we have order.

MR. STOKES, of Tennessee—I am authorized, Mr. President, by the delegation from Tennessee, to cast the vote of our State as a unit for Schuyler Colfax. [Applause.]

MR. WOOD, of Kentucky—Mr. President, I am authorized to cast the vote of Kentucky as a unit for Schuyler Colfax.

MR. LEE, of South Carolina—Mr. President, the delegation from South Carolina desires to change its vote to Schuyler Colfax. [Applause and confusion.]

THE PRESIDENT—It is impossible to transact any business until the Convention gets seated and returns to order. The work could be done in a minute, that now, in this way, cannot be done here in an hour. I am waiting to announce the vote given by South Carolina and Florida. I then will listen to gentlemen. South Carolina, I understood to give her vote unanimously for Mr. Colfax?

MR. LEE of South Carolina—That was the vote of South Carolina.

THE CHAIRMAN of the Florida delegation—Mr. President, I am instructed by the delegates from Florida to present a flowery tribute of six votes for Schuyler Colfax. [Applause.]

MR. BARKER, of Maine—I am instructed, Mr. President, by the delegation from Maine, to change its vote from its first choice to its second one, and give its fourteen votes for Schuyler Colfax. [Cheers.]

THE PRESIDENT—Maine announces its vote unanimously for Colfax.

THE CHAIRMAN of the Minnesota delegation—The whole delegation cast their vote for Colfax. [Applause.]

THE CHAIRMAN of the Wisconsin delegation—Mr. President, the delegation from Wisconsin has instructed me to cast their vote unanimously in favor of Schuyler Colfax. [Cheers.]

MR. JONES, of Ohio—Mr. President, on behalf of the delegation of Ohio, by unanimous consent, I rise to make a motion to terminate this contest, where we seem to struggle now, to concentrate upon the distinguished statesman from Indiana. Mr. President, a large majority in the Ohio delegation presented her favorite son, Benjamin F. Wade, and desired his nomination. But, sir, whether it be Wade, or whether it be Colfax, or whether it should have been the distinguished gentleman from Massachusetts, or from New York, or any other of the great names here presented, Ohio fights as she votes, though the Legislature have legislated that, if there be a challenge of a man, on account of a possible admixture of colored blood in the veins of his father, or his grandfather ("why don't you vote?")—we will still, Mr. President, in spite of this, carry the flag of victory. We will not forget our tens of thousands who have fallen for the cause of our liberty, nor will we forget the sufferings of those men, nor the tears of their wives and orphans. I move, therefore, sir, that the Rules be suspended, and Schuyler Colfax be declared unanimously nominated.

THE CHAIRMAN of the Mississippi delegation—I am directed by the delegates from Mississippi to have their votes changed, so that they will have fourteen votes for Schuyler Colfax. [Applause.]

MR. PIERCE, of Virginia—I am instructed, sir, by the delegation from Virginia, to cast twenty votes for Schuyler Colfax. [Applause.]

THE CHAIRMAN of the Nevada delegation—Mr. President, Nevada changes her vote to Schuyler Colfax. [Applause.]

THE CHAIRMAN of the Kansas delegation—Mr. President, Kansas changes her vote to Colfax. [Applause.]

MR. THAYER, of Nebraska—Mr. President, Nebraska desires to change her vote to Schuyler Colfax. [Applause.]

MR. JONES, of Ohio—Mr. President, does the Chair entertain my motion to suspend the Rules, and declare the nomination unanimous?

SEVERAL DELEGATES—"No! no!"

THE PRESIDENT—Gentlemen of the Convention—

A DELEGATE from California—California desires to change her vote to Schuyler Colfax. [Applause.]

THE PRESIDENT—The Chair claims the floor. The gentleman from Ohio moves to suspend the Rules and make the nomination of Schuyler Colfax unanimous.

A DELEGATE—I second the motion.

SEVERAL DELEGATES—Go on with the roll!

THE PRESIDENT—Gentlemen—

SEVERAL DELEGATES—Call the roll!

THE PRESIDENT—It requires two-thirds of the Convention to suspend the rules. The Chair decides that the roll must be called.

The Secretary then proceeded to call the roll.

THE SECRETARY—Alabama!

A DELEGATE from Alabama—Mr. President, Alabama casts fifteen votes for Colfax and one for Governor Fenton.

THE SECRETARY—Arkansas!

A DELEGATE from Arkansas—Mr. President, Arkansas casts ten votes for Colfax.

THE SECRETARY—California!

A DELEGATE from California—Mr. President, California casts ten votes for Colfax.

MR. COCHRANE, of New York—Mr. President, I rise for information. The delegates in this quarter of the Convention do not know, now, upon what business the Convention is engaged, or in what part of the call it is.

THE PRESIDENT—There was strong objection made to any suspension of the Rules, and, hearing no motion, the Chair decided, under the regular order of business, to call the roll again.

MR. COCHRANE, of New York—We ask, sir, for the announcement of the vote of—

THE PRESIDENT—The Chair will give the announcement of the vote.

MR. COCHRANE, of New York—That, sir, is in order, and nothing else is in order.

THE PRESIDENT—The Convention, it seemed to me, called for the call of the roll, because it would obviate the necessity of these changes, and I ordered it.

MR. PARKER, of New Jersey—Mr. President, a delegate from Maryland has been endeavoring, over and over again, to announce the vote of that State, but by some accident has not met your eye. I demand that he be heard.

THE PRESIDENT—The Convention has demanded the calling of the roll, in order to settle these changes. That is the better—

SEVERAL DELEGATES—Call the roll!

THE PRESIDENT—If the house prefer—

SEVERAL DELEGATES—Call the roll!

THE PRESIDENT—I now give the gentleman from Maryland the floor.

MR. SANDS, of Maryland—Mr. President, Maryland casts her vote of fourteen for Schuyler Colfax.

MR. COCHRANE, of New York—I rise, sir, for the information of the New York delegation. We understand that there is no new call for the roll, but a repetition, in order to certify to the old one ["That's it! That's it!"], so that, when a State is called, it is not for a new vote, but to ascertain and certify its old one, so that when New York may be called in its order, she is not to vote again, having on this very call cast her vote for Reuben E. Fenton. Am I right?

THE PRESIDENT—The Convention demanded the calling of the roll over again. The Chair hesitated a moment for that, and delegates again insisted that there should be a calling of the roll, from the beginning, to make these changes.

A DELEGATE—Mr. Chairman—

THE PRESIDENT—If there be no objection, the Chair will order the action; if not, the call will be proceeded with.

MR. COCHRANE, of New York—I hope, sir, the Chair will proceed in the usual way, and have the corrections made.

THE PRESIDENT—The Chair will order the usual course.

MR. ———, of North Carolina—Mr. President, North Carolina desires to change her eighteen votes to Schuyler Colfax. [Applause.]

MR. ———, of the District of Columbia—The District of Columbia desires to change her two votes to Schuyler Colfax.

MR. BROWN, of Georgia—Mr. President, the delegation from Georgia came here to support the choice of the Northern States, so soon as that choice should be manifest to us. I am, therefore, instructed by the delegation, to change the vote of Georgia, and cast eighteen votes for Schuyler Colfax. [Cries of "Good! good!"]

THE CHAIRMAN of the New Hampshire delegation—The delegation from New Hampshire desire that I should change the New Hampshire ten votes, and cast them for Schuyler Colfax. [Applause.]

MR. ———, of California—Mr. President, California desires to change her ten votes to Schuyler Colfax. [Applause.]

MR. THAYER, of Nebraska—Mr. President, Nebraska desires to change her vote and make it unanimous for Schuyler Colfax. [Applause.]

MR. PROUTY, of Kansas—Mr. President, Kansas desires to make her vote unanimous for Schuyler Colfax. [Applause.]

THE CHAIRMAN of the Arkansas delegation—Mr. President, Arkansas desires to make her vote unanimous for Schuyler Colfax. [Applause.]

THE CHAIRMAN of the Texas delegation—Texas casts her twelve votes for Colfax. [Cheers.]

MR. SCHURZ, of Missouri—Missouri desires to make her vote unanimous for Schuyler Colfax. [Applause.]

THE CHAIRMAN of the Delaware delegation—Mr. President, Delaware is unanimous for Schuyler Colfax. [Cheers.]

MR. HARRIS, of West Virginia—Mr. President, West Virginia desires to make her ten votes unanimous for Schuyler Colfax. [Cheers.]

THE PRESIDENT—Gentlemen of the Convention, have you made all the changes you desire?

SEVERAL DELEGATES—"New York!" "New York!"

MR. MCCLURE, of Pennsylvania—At an early period, when the name of Pennsylvania was called, she cast her votes for Colfax and Wade. At a subsequent period we changed it so as to make it unanimous—our fifty-two votes are cast for Schuyler Colfax. I didn't know whether you had heard it corrected or not. On behalf of Pennsylvania, I beg leave to say that it will uphold any Republican ticket that may be presented this fall, notwithstanding you have omitted to give us our first choice—Governor Curtin. [Great applause.]

A DELEGATE from Nevada—Mr. President—

THE PRESIDENT—If there be no more changes to make on this vote, the Secretary will give the summary as soon as possible.

THE DELEGATE from Nevada—Mr. President, I wish to announce that Nevada has changed her vote. [Applause.]

MR. LOGAN, of Illinois—I desire that Illinois may be called. Illinois gives thirty-two votes for Schuyler Colfax, of Indiana. [Applause.]

[Calls for "New York!" etc., and "music!"]

The following is the final vote, after changes:

FINAL BALLOT.

STATES.	No. of Delegates.	Fenton.	Wade.	Colfax.
Alabama	18	1	......	15
Arkansas	10	......	......	10
California	10	......	......	10
Colorado	6	......	......	6
Connecticut	12	......	......	12
Dakota	2	......	......	2
Delaware	6	......	......	6
District of Columbia	2	......	......	2
Florida	6	......	......	6
Georgia	18	......	......	18
Idaho	2	2	......	.....
Illinois	32	......	......	32
Indiana	26	......	......	26
Iowa	16	......	......	16
Kansas	6	......	......	6
Kentucky	22	......	......	22
Louisiana	14	......	......	14
Maine	14	......	......	14
Maryland	14	......	......	14
Massachusetts	24	......	......	24
Michigan	16	......	......	16
Minnesota	8	......	......	8
Mississippi	14	......	......	14
Missouri	22	......	......	22
Montana	2	......	2	.....
Nebraska	6	......	......	6
Nevada	6	......	......	6
New Hampshire	10	......	......	10
New Jersey	14	......	......	14
New York	66	66	......	.....
North Carolina	18	......	......	18
Ohio	42	......	36	6
Oregon	6	......	......	6
Pennsylvania	52	......	......	52
Rhode Island	8	......	......	8
South Carolina	12	......	......	12
Tennessee	20	......	......	20
Texas	12	......	......	12
Vermont	10	......	......	10
Virginia	20	......	......	20
West Virginia	10	......	......	10
Wisconsin	16	......	......	16
Total	650	69	38	541

COLFAX DECLARED NOMINATED.

THE PRESIDENT—I will read the statement of the vote:

The whole number of votes cast	648
Necessary to a choice	325
Schuyler Colfax, of Indiana, has	541
R. E. Fenton, of New York, has	69
B. F. Wade, of Ohio, has	38

You have made the choice of the Hon. Schuyler Colfax, of Indiana. [Tremendous and prolonged applause. [Cries, "New York! New York."]

THE NOMINATION MADE UNANIMOUS.

MR. SICKLES, of New York—Mr. President, I need not say, and no one will need to be assured, that New York stands true to her colors. We have clung to our candidate, Gov. Fenton, with the same tenacity with which our constituents have always adhered to the Republican cause. [Cheers.] The time has come, however, when we have to prove that we are not less mindful than our sister States, of what we owe to the harmony of the action of the Convention. [Prolonged applause.] Ardently as we desired, and confidently as we anticipated, the nomination of our favorite candidate, we bow to the wisdom of the Convention, and accept the choice which is made. In obedience to the instructions of the New York delegation, and in accordance with my own sentiments, I now move that the nomination of Schuyler Colfax, as our candidate for the Vice Presidency, be made unanimous. [Great applause.]

MR. ———, of Indiana—I call for three cheers for the "one-legged General."

The cheers were given.

Three cheers were then called for Governor Fenton, and three cheers for Senator Wilson, which were also given.

MR. JONES, of Ohio—Was there ever such a race as this, in which Ohio had the leading nag in the race, and nearly had the leading horse on the home stretch, and yet is denied the poor privilege of congratulating the winner? I hope the Convention will allow the Empire State of the West to have the poor privilege of joining the Empire State of the East in seconding the nomination. [Cheers.]

A delegate called for three cheers for Ohio, and another called for three cheers for Ben. Wade, which were given.

MR. ——, of Louisiana—I am instructed to propose three cheers for the Ticket.

The cheers were given.

THE PRESIDENT—You have heard the motion of the gentleman from New York, seconded by the gentleman from Ohio, that the nomination of Schuyler Colfax for Vice President of the United States be made unanimous. Those who are in favor of the motion, say "aye."

The motion prevailed unanimously.

THE PRESIDENT—There is nobody left. [Laughter.] We need not call for the noes, Schuyler Colfax is the nominee of the Convention! [Applause.]

DESPATCH FROM MR. COLFAX.

THE PRESIDENT—I have an important despatch to read. It is one in which you will doubtless be much interested. It is addressed by the Hon. Schuyler Colfax, to the Hon. J. B. Defrees, of Indiana, and he says:

"I read this morning to General Grant, the midnight despatch, giving an abstract of the platform, and General Grant heartily approves its tone." [Great applause.]

Gentlemen, it will be necessary to call the roll of States, for the purpose of ascertaining who have been selected as members of the National Committee.

COMMITTEE TO WAIT ON THE CANDIDATES.

MR. SICKLES, of New York—Mr. President, before the roll is called for that purpose, I desire to submit a motion. I move that the officers of this Convention constitute a Committee, to communicate to our candidates for President and Vice President their nomination by this Convention.

MR. COCHRANE, of New York—Mr. President, I second the motion.

MR. ——, of ——I understand, Mr. President, it to be the rule, that a Committee nominated by the delegates from each State, is selected for that duty. [Cries of "No!" etc.]

THE PRESIDENT—The officers are chosen from each State, a Secretary and Vice President, from each State, and the States are thus represented.

The motion prevailed.

MR. SICKLES—I wish it to be understood, as a part of my motion, that they communicate the Platform and Proceedings of this Convention, also.

THE PRESIDENT—The Convention has so understood it.

MR. ——, of South Carolina—I move you a vote of thanks to the officers of the Convention, for the manner in which they have presided over this business.

MR. VAN ZANDT, of Rhode Island—The roll should be called first.

NATIONAL EXECUTIVE COMMITTEE.

The Secretary then called the States, and the following was announced as the National Executive Committee:

Alabama—Jas. P. Stowe.
Arkansas—B. F. Rice.
California—Geo. C. Gorham.
Colorado—Daniel Witter.
Connecticut—H. H. Starkweather.
Dakota—Newton Edmunds.
Delaware—Edward G. Bradford.
District of Columbia—S. E. Bowen.
Florida—S. B. Conover.
Georgia—J. H. Caldwell.
Idaho—John C. Henly.
Illinois—J. Russel Jones.
Indiana—Cyrus M. Allen.
Iowa—Josiah Tracy.
Kansas—John A. Martin.
Kentucky—Allen A. Burton.
Louisiana—M. H. Southworth.
Maine—Lewis Barker.
Maryland—Charles C. Fulton.
Massachusetts—William Claflin.
Michigan—Marsh Giddings.
Minnesota—John T. Averill.
Mississippi—A. C. Fisk.
Missouri—Benj. F. Loan.
Montana—Lester S. Wilson.
Nebraska—E. B. Taylor.
Nevada—Charles E. DeLong.
New Hampshire—Wm. E. Chandler.
New Jersey—J. Gobsill.
New York—Horace Greeley.
North Carolina—William Sloane.
Ohio—B. R. Cowen.
Oregon—H. W. Corbett.
Pennsylvania—Wm. H. Kemble.
Rhode Island—Lyman B. Frieze.
South Carolina—James H. Jenks.
Tennessee—Wm. B. Stokes.
Texas—A. J. Hamilton.
Vermont—T. W. Park.
Virginia—Franklin Stearns.
West Virginia—Samuel D. Karns.
Wisconsin—David Atwood.

MEETING OF THE COMMITTEE.

THE PRESIDENT—Gentlemen of the Convention: I am requested to announce that the National Committee will meet at the Tremont House to-night, at 8½ o'clock, to organize.

VOTE OF THANKS.

THE CHAIRMAN of the Nevada Delegation—Mr. President I move you that the thanks of this Convention be returned to the officers thereof.

The motion was unanimously adopted.

MR. COCHRANE, of New York—Mr. President, I move you, sir, that the thanks of this Convention, for the ability, labor and courtesy of the Committee of Arrangements, be bestowed upon the Committee by the Convention.

The motion prevailed unanimously.

MR. COCHRANE, of New York—It is understood, sir, I suppose, that the proceedings of the Convention, as furnished by the Official Reporters of this Convention, will be duly signed by the officers of the Convention and published; if not, I make a motion to that effect.

THE PRESIDENT—The proceedings will be so published.

A DELEGATE—I move that the thanks of this Convention be tendered to the former National Executive Committee.

The motion prevailed.

ADJOURNMENT.

MR. COCHRANE, of New York—If there be no further business, I move the Convention do now adjourn *sine die.*

A VOICE—"Not *sine die.*"

MR. COCHRANE, of New York—I suggest that it be at the call of the National Executive Committee, Mr. President.

The motion prevailed,

And the Convention stood adjourned subject to the call of the National Executive Committee.

CALL FOR GOVERNOR HAWLEY.

A delegate called for three cheers for the President of the Convention, Governor Hawley, which were given.

Loud cries were then made for General Hawley, who stepped forward and responded, as follows:

GENTLEMEN: Perhaps it is thrown away to say to you that it must be an impossibility for any person to speak now, after the labors of the day, and, I think, quite as nearly impossible, for any person to listen. I thank you for the compliment of the call. I shall save all my strength of body and mind for the campaign, for from now until the day of election I shall either write editorials or take the stump, and, hence, I am satisfied you will excuse me. [Prolonged applause.]

NATIONAL EXECUTIVE COMMITTEE, 1868.

Alabama—James P. Stowe, Montgomery.
Arkansas—B. F. Rice, Little Rock.
California—George G. Gorham, San Francisco.
Colorado—Daniel Witter, Denver.
Connecticut—H. H. Starkweather, Norwich.
Dakota—Newton Edmunds, Yankton.
Delaware—Edward C. Bradford.
District of Columbia—Sayles E. Bowen, Washington.
Florida—S. B. Conover, Lake City.
Georgia—John H. Caldwell, Lagrange.
Idaho—J. C. Henly.
Illinois—J. Russell Jones, Chicago.
Indiana—Cyrus M. Allen, Vincennes.
Iowa—Josiah Tracy, Burlington.
Kansas—John A. Martin, Atchison.
Kentucky—Allen A. Burton, Lancaster.
Louisiana—M. H. Southworth, New Orleans.
Maine—Louis Barker, Stetson
Maryland—Chas. C. Fulton, Baltimore.
Massachusetts—Wm. Claflin, Boston.
Michigan—Marsh Giddings, Kalamazoo.
Minnesota—J. T. Averill, St. Paul.
Mississippi—A. C. Fisk, Vicksburg.
Missouri—Benj. F. Loan, St. Joseph.
Montana—Lester S. Wilson, Bozeman City.
Nebraska—E. B. Taylor, Omaha.
Nevada—Chas. E. De Long, Virginia City.
New Hampshire—Wm. E. Chandler, Washington, D. C.
New Jersey—James Gobsill, Jersey City.
New York—Horace Greeley, New York City.
North Carolina—W. Sloane.
Ohio—B. R. Cowen, Bellaire.
Oregon—H. W. Corbett, Washington, D. C.
Pennsylvania—W. H. Kemble, Philadelphia.
Rhode Island—Lyman B. Frieze, Providence.
South Carolina—James H. Jenks, Charleston.
Tenessee—W. B. Stokes, Liberty.
Texas—A. J. Hamilton.
Vermont—T. W. Park, Bennington.
Virginia—Franklin Stearns.
West Virginia—Samuel D. Karns, Parkersburg.
Wisconsin—David Atwood, Madison.

ORGANIZATION

OF

NATIONAL EXECUTIVE COMMITTEE.

At a meeting of the National Executive Committee, an organization was effected, as follows:

HON. WM. CLAFLIN, CHAIRMAN.
HON. WM. E. CHANDLER, SECRETARY.

CENTRAL EXECUTIVE COMMITTEE.

(Headquarters at New York City.)

WM. CLAFLIN, CHAIRMAN.

HORACE GREELEY,	T. W. PARK,	MARSH GIDDINGS,
WM. H. KEMBLE,	R. R. COWEN,	H. H. STARKWEATHER,

EXECUTIVE COMMITTEE FOR THE WEST.

(Headquarters at Chicago.)

J. RUSSELL JONES, CYRUS M. ALLEN, E. B. TAYLOR.

EXECUTIVE COMMITTEE FOR THE SOUTH.

(Headquarters at Atlanta, Georgia.)

M. H. SOUTHWORTH, B. F. RICE, JOHN H. CALDWELL.

EXECUTIVE COMMITTEE FOR THE PACIFIC COAST.

(Headquarters at San Francisco.)

GEO. C. GORHAM, CHAS. E. DELONG.

LETTER OF ACCEPTANCE.

FROM SCHUYLER COLFAX.

"WASHINGTON, D. C., May 30, 1850.

"HON. J. R. HAWLEY,

"*President of the National Union Republican Convention:*

"DEAR SIR: The platform adopted by the patriotic convention over which you presided, and the resolutions which so happily supplement it, so entirely agree with my views as to a just national policy, that my thanks are due to the delegates as much for this clear and auspicious declaration of principles, as for the nomination with which I have been honored, and which I gratefully accept.

"When a great rebellion, which imperiled the national existence, was at last overthrown, the duty of all others, devolving upon those intrusted with the responsibilities of legislation, evidently was to require that the revolted States should be re-admitted to participation in the government against which they had erred only on such a basis as to increase and fortify, not to weaken or endanger, the strength and power of the nation. Certainly no one ought to have claimed that they should be re-admitted under such rule that their organization as States could ever again be used, as at the opening of the war, to defy the national authority or to destroy the national unity. This principle has been the pole star of those who have inflexibly insisted on the Congressional policy your Convention so cordially indorsed.

"Baffled by Executive opposition and by persistent refusals to accept any plan of reconstruction proffered by Congress, justice and public safety at last combined to teach us that only by an enlargement of suffrage in those States could the desired end be attained, and that it was even more safe to give the ballot to those who loved the Union than to those who had sought ineffectually to destroy it. The assured success of this legislation is being written on the adamant of history, and will be our triumphant vindication. More clearly, too, than ever before does the nation now recognize that the greatest glory of a Republic is, that it throws the shield of its protection over the humblest and weakest of its people, and vindicates the rights of the poor and the powerless as faithfully as those of the rich and the powerful.

"I rejoice, too, in this connection, to find in your platform the frank and fearless avowal that naturalized citizens must be protected abroad "at every hazard, as though they were native born." Our whole people are foreigners, or descendants of foreigners. Our fathers established by arms their right to be called a

LETTER OF ACCEPTANCE.

FROM U. S. GRANT.

"To General John R. Hawley,

"*President National Union Republican Convention:*

"In formally accepting the nomination of the National Union Republican Convention of the 21st of May instant, it seems proper that some statement of views beyond the mere acceptance of the nomination should be expressed. The proceedings of the Convention were marked with wisdom, moderation and patriotism, and I believe express the feelings of the great mass of those who sustained the country through its recent trials.

"I endorse the resolutions. If elected to the office of President of the United States it will be my endeavor to administer all the laws in good faith, with economy, and with the view of giving peace, quiet and protection everywhere.

"In times like the present it is impossible, or at least eminently improper, to lay down a policy to be adhered to, right or wrong, through an administration of four years. New political issues, not foreseen, are constantly arising; the views of the public on old ones are constantly changing, and a purely administrative officer should always be left free to execute the will of the people. I always have respected that will, and always shall.

"Peace and universal prosperity—its sequence,—with economy of administration, will lighten the burden of taxation, while it constantly reduces the national debt. Let us have peace.

"With great respect, your obedient servant,

"U. S. GRANT.

"Washington, May 29, 1868."

nation. It remains for us to establish the right to welcome to our shores all who are willing, by oaths of allegiance, to become American citizens. Perpetual allegiance, as claimed abroad, is only another name for perpetual bondage, and would make all slaves to the soil where first they saw the light. Our national cemeteries prove how faithfully these oaths of fidelity to their adopted land have been sealed in the life-blood of thousands upon thousands. Should we then be faithful to the dead, if we did not protect their living brethren in the full enjoyment of that nationality, for which, side by side with the native born, our soldiers of foreign birth laid down their lives ?

"It was fitting, too, that the representatives of a party which had proved so true to national duty in time of war, should speak so clearly in time of peace for the maintenance untarnished of the national honor, national credit and good faith as regards its debt, the cost of our national existence.

"I do not need to extend this reply by further comment on a platform which has elicited such hearty approval throughout the land. The debt of gratitude it acknowledges to the brave men who saved the Union from destruction, the frank approval of amnesty based on repentance and loyalty, the demand for the most thorough economy and honesty in the government, the sympathy of the party of liberty with all throughout the world who long for the liberty we here enjoy, and the recognition of the sublime principles of the Declaration of Independence, are worthy of the organization on whose banners they are to be written in the coming contest. Its past record cannot be blotted out or forgotten. If there had been no Republican party, slavery would to-day cast its baneful shadow over the Republic. If there had been no Republican party, a free press and free speech would be as unknown from the Potomac to the Rio Grande as ten years ago. If the Republican party could have been stricken from existence when the banner of rebellion was unfurled, and when the response of "no coercion" was heard at the North, we would have had no nation to-day. But for the Republican party daring to risk the odium of tax and draft laws our flag could not have been kept flying in the field until the long-hoped-for victory came. Without a Republican party the Civil Rights bill—the guaranty of equality under the law to the humble and the defenceless, as well as to the strong—would not be to-day upon our national statute book.

"With such inspiration from the past, and following the example of the founders of the Republic, who called the victorious General of the Revolution to preside over the land his triumphs had saved from its enemies, I cannot doubt that our labors will be crowned with success. And it will be a success that will bring restored hope, confidence, prosperity and progress, South as well as North, West as well as East, and, above all, the blessings, under Providence, of national Concord and Peace.

"Very truly yours,

"SCHUYLER COLFAX."

www.ingramcontent.com/pod-product-compliance
Lightning Source LLC
LaVergne TN
LVHW021414110826
845150LV00007B/1916

* 9 7 8 1 4 2 5 5 1 0 4 6 6 *